How to Guide

Patrons, Presidents and Personalities

Working with high-level volunteers

Eileen Hammond

DIRECTORY OF SOCIAL CHANGE

In association with
the Institute of Fundraising

Published by
Directory of Social Change
24 Stephenson Way
London NW1 2DP
Tel. 08450 77 77 07; Fax 020 7391 4804
Email publications@dsc.org.uk
www.dsc.org.uk
from whom further copies and a full books catalogue are available.

Directory of Social Change is a Registered Charity no. 800517

First published 2008

ISBN 978 1 903991 98 5

British Library Cataloguing in Publication Data

A catalogue record for this book is available from the British Library.

Cover and text designed by Kate Bass
Typeset by Keystroke, Wolverhampton
Printed and bound by Page Bros, Norwich

All Directory of Social Change departments in London:
08450 77 77 07

Directory of Social Change Northern Office:
Research 0151 708 0136

Contents

To Alan for his loving support and encouragement to write this book and for his endurance of 40 years of marriage to a fundraiser

Acknowledgements

Jonathan Anscombe	Contact a Family
Laura Bennett	Information Officer, Volunteering England
Susan Brumpton	Chief Executive, MERU
Sue Burch	Marketing and Communications, MERU
Max Clifford	Max Clifford Associates
Bridget Cluley	Bridget Cluley Associates
Mike Denny	Fundraising Director, Oakhaven Hospice Trust
Ava Easton	Development Manager, Encephalitis Society
Derek Farr	Manager, Action in Mental Health
Serena Greaves	Artist Development Manager, Barnado's
Pamela Gregory	Fundraising and Media Manager, Age Concern Surrey
Liz Haigh-Reeve	Director of Fundraising, The Children's Trust
Sophie Isachsen	Clarence House Press Office
Rob Jackson	Director of Volunteering Development, Volunteering England
Nina Kapur	Head of PR and Communications, Breakthrough Breast Cancer
Martin Kemp	Film and TV Actor
Linda Laurance	Governance Consultant
Laurence Llewelyn-Bowen	Interior Design Consultant and TV Presenter
Hugo Middlemas	Director of Fundraising, Parkinson's Disease Society
Katrina Tanzer	PA to Celebrities
Tanya Winch	Celebrity and PR Manager, Breakthrough Breast Cancer

About the author

EILEEN HAMMOND has worked in the voluntary sector for 30 years from Area Organiser, and Appeals Director to Chief Executive. She has been involved in the development of a number of new charities, where the recruitment of Patrons, Presidents and celebrities was an important part of raising the profile of the charity to a wider audience. Throughout that time she has also worked as a volunteer for youth organisations, directed amateur musical productions and served periods as President of both local Inner Wheel and Soroptimist Clubs.

A Fellow of the Institute of Fundraising, Eileen is a past Honorary Secretary and currently a member of the Standards Committee which develops the codes of practice for the sector. She is also a Director of the Association of Fundraising Consultants and a Professional Adviser on the Board of Trustees of Barts and The London Charity. With husband Alan, she is now a partner in the charity consultancy, Hammond Associates.

Foreword

As someone who has worked closely with Patrons, Presidents, and Personalities for over 30 years, I am impressed at how Eileen Hammond has tackled this significant and important area of charity work. My work in the Charity Communications and Fundraising world has always greatly benefited from working with influential people, getting them to help raise funds, enthuse about the cause, and bring new supporters to the organisation.

I am still making new friends and contacts in those areas Eileen has written about because I have seen the results that can be achieved through these relationships. Both NCH and the British Red Cross would be poorer in monetary and promotional terms without having Presidents, Patrons and Personalities, as would many other Charities who value and respect the tremendous support given by these volunteers who 'make a difference'.

I commend Eileen's book to all those of us engaged in Charitable events, PR programmes and fundraising. The book is a real learning tool and should be read.

JOHN F GRAY

John is co-author of *Organising Special Events* published by DSC, a founder and Fellow of the Institute of Fundraising and Fellow of the Chartered Institute of Public Relations.

He is past Director of Communications and Fundraising for NCH and the British Red Cross and is now the Chief Executive of UCLH Charitable Foundation.

Introduction

Imagine the scene: a tavern in London in the year 1865. Two men are seated at a table engaged in earnest discussion when they are joined by a third man with a literary air about him. The conversation, as is common in such establishments, turns to the problems of the age – poverty, the homeless, abandoned children and the host of evils which have blighted society to varying degrees at every stage of its development.

The feature which distinguishes their discussions from those of others around them in the crowded inn is that these three men set in train initiatives which made an immeasurable difference to people whose lives were blighted by the misery and hardship of the social conditions of the day; practical, effective measures that are still saving and improving lives in the twenty-first century.

The three men were the 7th Earl of Shaftesbury, Dr Thomas Barnado and Charles Dickens and, although the meeting described is imaginary, their respective contributions to improvement in social conditions are well known: the charitable establishments founded by the first two and the raising of public awareness brought about by the writings of the third.

What had they in common? First, they were all three passionately concerned, not just about the misery and injustice they saw around them, but also about the need to do something about it. Second, unlike the majority of their contemporaries in the tavern, they were well-known, influential figures in society and, because of this, they were in a position to enlist powerful allies and to organise concerted action in a way which would make a real and sustained difference to the lives of those they sought to help. They were, in short, personalities whom people knew, admired, trusted and were willing to follow.

Today every charity understands the importance of high-profile figures in raising public awareness of its cause and the funds necessary to carry out its work. But among the glittering array of public personalities, who would be the most suitable match for our charity? How do we find them? If we're successful in landing them, what do we do with them? Should we make them patrons or presidents and what's the difference? How do we sustain the relationship? These and many other questions can pose real problems, particularly for smaller or recently formed charities that may have little experience or understanding of how to approach high-profile figures, or of how to use their services effectively, and who frequently have an unrealistic expectation of what such affiliations can achieve for their cause.

Recently, I was approached by the trustees of a comparatively newly established charity who, having set up the necessary governance structure and appointed staff, wanted advice on the subject of patrons and presidents. A meeting was arranged during which it became clear that they expected a brief explanation of what a charity should have in terms of high-level volunteer involvement and a few tips on how to go about getting it – a sort of one-size-fits-all solution. I explained that every charity is unique and that their own requirements would depend upon a number of factors which would need careful consideration. In order to save further consultancy time and cost, I suggested that the best course was to refer them to an appropriate book which would introduce them to the subject and give practical advice on how to proceed. At the end of our meeting, we agreed that I would do some research and let them know of a suitable publication.

However, a search among the lengthy lists of published works on almost every aspect of fundraising revealed a notable absence of any book exclusively about the recruitment and involvement of personalities as patrons, presidents or other high-profile roles in charities.

So here it is.

1

Patrons and presidents

- Leading figures
- Why do we need them?
- When do we need them?
- What's the difference?
- Other leading roles

Leading figures

We all have a pretty good idea of the role of a Chief Executive. Whether the charity is large or small, national or local, the function of the chief executive's office is fundamentally the same. Similarly, the Director of Fundraising, the Finance Director and the Head of Operations are all entrusted with tasks which are implicit in their titles – although those titles may vary slightly from charity to charity. However, there is no such clarity about the roles of Patrons and Presidents or the differences between them. Among the top fifty charities by voluntary income, there are some that have one Patron, others that have well over a hundred; some have a President or Presidents but no Patron; others have a list of Vice-Presidents but no President. There are still other charities that function perfectly well without Patrons and/or Presidents.

At first sight this seems a bewildering maze of inconsistency badly in need of some standardisation. Yet it works. The charity world has never subscribed to the principle of conformity; indeed, every charity was brought into existence to make changes to the existing order of things in order to right a wrong or to meet a need. And they do that, not by conforming to a norm but by taking innovative measures relevant to their own particular objectives. So this diversity of practice regarding Patrons and Presidents should be seen as an aspect of the freedom each charitable organisation has to organise its affairs in the way it deems most effective in the achievement of its aims.

Why do we need them?

The one thing that can be stated with certainty is that charities benefit from association with leading figures – that is, 'personalities' – who are known either to the general public or to the specific section of the public which is of interest to a particular charity and who may be seen as role models whose example others are willing to follow.

Similarly, individuals who are capable of instilling this trust in others can themselves benefit from association with charitable causes. It is interesting to speculate upon how many charities are thriving today because of their famous founders and how many founders became famous because of the charitable causes they espoused. This indicates a symbiotic relationship between charities and their leading figures who, in this book, are referred to generically as 'Personalities'.

There are stages in the lives and careers of politicians, rock stars, authors, sportsmen, film stars, TV personalities and so on, when they would welcome being associated with a charitable cause. Similarly, charities experience times when the need for credibility, status, public awareness and trust becomes a matter of great importance. Before going on to consider the specific roles that personalities can usefully fill in charitable organisations, we should perhaps look at the optimum timing for charities to become active in seeking the involvement of high-level volunteers.

When do we need them?

The trustees of a former client charity that I had helped during their rather challenging formative years were experiencing difficulties in relating to their chairman. One solution they suggested (in his absence) was that they 'promote' him to be Patron of the charity, thus freeing them to appoint another chairman and at the same time providing a Patron to fill the vacant space on their letterhead.

I was obliged to point out two major flaws in this proposal. First, was he an ideal candidate for the role of Patron? Second, what would they do if they had the opportunity of acquiring a more suitable candidate for the position? The charity was at a crossroads in its development and it was the right time to consider creating roles which could give a lead to the charity beyond that which had been achieved by the founding trustees. However, it was essential that such appointments were made only after careful consideration of where the charity wished to position itself in the public eye, rather than as a knee-jerk reaction to solving the immediate problem as it had initially been perceived.

In fact, that particular difficulty was resolved quite simply when they took up my suggestion and invited him to become a vice-president, along with a few others, thus giving them time to think more strategically about other high-profile roles for the future. But it does highlight the need to look at our organisations objectively and to decide whether the time is right to enlist high-profile figures to help carry us forward.

In most cases, charities are initially set up by committed individuals who have an awareness of an urgent need and the passion to set about meeting it. And that's the way it should be. Whether the founders are well known to the public or not, their commitment to the cause will see them through. At that early stage, the absence of a high-level patron or president is not essential – though it could help!

But most fledgling charities soon find that theirs is a very small voice in a very large and noisy environment and, in order to make themselves known to the people 'out there', they must grow bigger and more noticeable. The need for funding may be pressing; if they are a campaigning organisation, their message has to be communicated; the public has to be made aware of the importance of their cause. In such circumstances, they need a voice which can be heard and this could be supplied by a Personality to whom the public will listen and whose example they will follow.

Periods of growth, particularly in the early stages of a charity's life, are exhilarating. Waves of public support for the cause are a source of inspiration for staff and volunteers alike, motivating them to go the extra mile. Later on, as the charity grows, there are, inevitably, periods of staleness and, at such times, an injection of new blood with its attendant publicity can be just what's needed to rally the troops.

In another sense, it could be said that the best time to recruit Personalities is when the charity is riding high. A successful and active organisation is a far more attractive prospect than one whose staff is demotivated and whose trustees are becoming tired and less inclined to devote time and energy to a cause that they may feel is making little progress.

As we shall see later, another key consideration in deciding when to approach a particular individual is that of timing, which is also important to Personalities. They too have high points and low points in their lives and their careers, and they are more likely to respond to your request if it fits in well with their own plans and aspirations.

Still, whenever the appropriate time comes to think about bringing high-profile Personalities on board, it is important to be clear as to what is meant by Patrons and Presidents. As we've seen, charities differ widely in their interpretation of these terms but there are certain core principles that can be used to guide and inform your discussions about what is right for your particular organisation.

What's the difference?

Patrons

The *Concise Oxford Dictionary* defines a patron as (among other things) 'a distinguished person who takes an honorary position in a charity'. Unlike trustees, patrons have no legal status or binding obligations. Neither do they have any responsibility for the management of the organisation or the manner in which funds are spent. Their role is, in most cases, that of a 'figurehead' or 'flag bearer', a leader whose example people are willing to follow and whose name can lend credibility and status to the organisation which, in turn, can increase the effectiveness of its fundraising, campaigning and public relations activities. A distinguished patron can also, in certain circumstances, provide high-level entry to powerful organisations and institutions, to which the charity might not otherwise have access.

While, if chosen with careful consideration, a patron can be a great asset to a charity on an ongoing and developing basis, in most cases, his or her role demands little 'hands-on' involvement. Their sympathy with the cause and approval of the charity's work is demonstrated publicly by their name on the letterhead and reinforced by the occasional appearance at an event.

In many cases, the appointment of a patron (particularly a member of the Royal Family) is on an ongoing and more or less permanent basis and the charity benefits from the resultant sense of continuity and stability.

Some charities have a cautious attitude to the appointment of patrons, believing that there may be a possibility of the appointee becoming too actively involved and thereby creating, in effect, an additional tier of management. Chief executives, for instance, who have learned to deal effectively with their trustees, may be reluctant to begin the same process with patrons. Nonetheless, it is the case that most patrons are content to allow the use of their name and therefore, by implication, their support and approval without becoming physically involved in the charities' activities. Any fears concerning excessive or unwanted involvement in the charity's affairs can be allayed by the process of giving careful consideration to the manner of appointment and the form of the agreement between charity and patron.

However, some charities make a number of appointments, drawing a distinction between 'The Patron' and other patrons who can be asked to support a particular campaign or help raise the profile of the charity for a limited period.

Presidents

'The Head of a Society, council or other organisation.' This definition (again taken from the *Concise Oxford Dictionary*) makes clear that the role of a president is a more 'hands-on' role than that of a patron. Because of this, it is important that the person appointed should have credibility and relevance within the area of the charity's core activity, thus enhancing the charity's profile among appropriate audiences. An example of this is provided by The Encephalitis Society whose Patron, Martin Kemp, brings the charity to the attention of the media and the general public, while their recently appointed President, Professor Barbara Wilson OBE, brings the gravitas and professional credibility that the charity needs within the medical profession.

The distinction between the roles of trustees and presidents is very important. Very occasionally, the governing document of a charity will stipulate that the president should also fulfil the role of chair of the board of trustees. Governance consultant, Linda Laurance, advises that, in such cases, it is essential to identify which 'hat' is being worn and when, since he or she will carry all the responsibilities of trusteeship when acting in the role of chair, but not when acting in their capacity as president.

It would seem that in practice the roles of patron and president can be very similar – it is down to the individual charity to decide whether they have a patron or a president or sometimes both. The majority of charities have patrons and rather fewer have presidents.

Other leading roles

It is clear from the above that, although there are certain characteristics which distinguish the roles of patron and president, there is a good deal of overlap and, in the final analysis, it is up to your charity to decide which of these roles could usefully be filled – and by whom.

There are, of course, situations in which it may be inappropriate to seek to appoint a patron and/or a president. A charity may, for instance, feel that it is not yet ready to commit to taking such a step but nevertheless wishes to formalise a relationship with a leading figure or well-known personality in order to lend weight to a particular project. Alternatively, a charity may already have a patron or president but wish to recognise the ongoing support of some-one by giving a title to their role without appearing to detract from the importance of their patron/president.

In such cases, there is no reason why other titles should not be used. The choice would depend upon the nature of the charity's work and the particular role in question. A few examples are:

- **Vice-presidents** – This title carries a suitable degree of gravitas to be taken seriously and many charities appoint large numbers of vice-presidents – NSPCC, for example can boast (at the time of going to press) 22, and Save the Children enjoys the support of 31.
- **Ambassadors** – International charity UNICEF pioneered the use of celebrities in this role, beginning with Danny Kaye as their ambassador-at-large in 1954, followed by Audrey Hepburn and others and building to a very impressive list of international, regional and national goodwill ambassadors. The offer of this title can be a way of recruiting suitable people as well as a means of thanking people and recognising their contribution to, perhaps, fundraising or profile-raising.
- **Advocates, champions** – The possibilities are limitless – be creative! A title that is unusual or eye-catching can help to mark your charity out from others. Why not hold a brainstorming session with a view to inventing a title that embodies your charity's particular ethos and could be bestowed upon those whose involvement has made a significant difference?

Perhaps the most important thing to remember in making high-level appointments is that, whatever the title, there must be clarity on all sides as to what the role involves. The charity must be clear in its approach as to what is needed (and therefore, by implication, what is not needed) and the personality must be fully aware of the nature and extent of his or her expected involvement.

If carefully chosen and fully briefed, a patron or president should be an invaluable asset and if the relationship is properly managed the benefits to both charity and personality can increase as time goes by. On the other hand, an uncommitted or badly briefed incumbent of either role can, at best, be a hindrance and, at worst, devalue the cause.

Look after your personalities, whatever role they fill, and they will look after you.

Checklist for patrons and presidents

- Patrons do not have any legal responsibilities
- Patrons have no responsibility for management of the charity
- The patron has a minimal involvement on a regular basis
- A president is the head of an organisation
- Presidents must have credibility and relevance to the charity's work
- Badly informed leading figures can devalue the cause
- In practice the roles of patron and president can be very similar
- The majority of charities have patrons and fewer have presidents
- Some charities have neither patron nor president
- Other titles include vice-president, ambassador, champion

CASE STUDY

Barnado's

As well as its Royal Patron, HM The Queen, and Royal President, HRH The Duchess of Cornwall, Barnado's enjoys the services of no fewer than 21 vice-presidents drawn from a wide variety of fields including the media, business, religion and the world of celebrity. The charity's Artist Development Manager, Serena Greaves, explains that until 2004 many vice-presidents featured on the list for largely historic reasons, many from Christian faith backgrounds, and they were not required to play an active part in the work of the charity. Since then, however, the list has been reviewed, resulting in a reduction in numbers and a revitalisation of the role itself. Present holders of the title include author Leslie Thomas and fashion designer Bruce Oldfield, both of whom were, themselves, Barnardo's boys.

Prospective vice-presidents are now initially approached either in person or by letter and asked to consider taking on the role. Those who express an interest are invited to take part in discussions regarding their own particular skills, interests and time availability and, if a suitable role can be agreed upon, are appointed by the board of trustees and re-elected annually by the charity's members.

Barnado's seeks to draw its vice-presidents from a broad range of backgrounds, abilities and contacts in order to reflect the diversity of the charity's membership and service-users. The nature of their responsibilities will depend upon the amount of time which they are able or prepared to commit to the role and, while some may undertake only one or two engagements a year, others are able to offer much more time and play an important and active role in the organisation. The importance of time commitment is crucial and can prove to be a sticking point in initial discussions.

There is no written agreement with vice-presidents other than a letter setting out the charity's expectations and outlining the agreed basis upon which the post holder and the charity will work together.

The role of Barnardo's ambassadors, however, is less formal and very flexible. High-profile individuals who have already supported the charity in some way are approached in person and asked to consider taking on the role. As in the case of vice-presidents, the nature and extent of their support depend upon particular strengths, experience, knowledge and interests – and, of course, their availability which can vary considerably from year to year.

Examples of ways in which ambassadors can provide valuable assistance include 'opening doors' to useful contacts, lobbying on the charity's behalf for potential fundraising or other opportunities, acting as a spokesperson, supporting media campaigns, attending fundraising events, acting as a role model and inspiration to service-users by visiting projects, endorsing fundraising activities and so on. At the time of writing, Barnado's has four ambassadors: model Laura Bailey, actress Brenda Blethyn OBE, actress Michelle Collins and cricketer Kevin Pietersen MBE.

Many personalities can be unavailable for quite long periods of time through commitments such as filming and touring, and the nature of their work can mean that schedules change at short notice, making it difficult or impossible to commit themselves in advance. They may, nevertheless empathise with the work that Barnado's does and be willing to provide support as and when they can. Recognising this, Barnado's maintains a further pool of celebrity supporters who can be drawn on from time to time for a variety of purposes depending on their background, interests and availability.

Serena believes that 'the backing of established and well-known supporters is very valuable to Barnardo's in so many ways. They add weight and profile to our media campaigns and fundraising activities, and by their support and interest help inspire many of the young people with whom we work.'

In all, Barnado's provides a prime example of how the roles of vice-president and ambassador can be tailor-made to enlist the services of personalities whose involvement, together with the Royal Patron and President, can prove invaluable to the work of the charity, and how other personalities can also be involved on an ad hoc basis as their commitments permit.

2

Personalities

- What do we mean by 'personalities'?
- Celebrities – who needs them?
- The great and the good
- The Royal Family
- Other categories of personality
- Who's using whom?

When I moved from working for a local charity to become an area organiser with Save the Children more than 25 years ago, one of the major differences I noticed was how much easier it was to engage the interest of personalities because of the charity's high profile – due, in part, to its Royal president. At that time, associations between charities and famous people were perhaps less common than is the case now, when it would appear to be *de rigueur* to have a celebrity or two on board – it sometimes seems that ours is a celebrity-obsessed culture.

Yet the concept of high-profile figures lending their support to charitable causes is not new. Charles Dickens certainly did his bit to raise awareness of the plight of the poor in nineteenth-century London – much influenced, no doubt, by his contemporaries, Thomas Barnardo and Lord Shaftesbury. Indeed, in the modern sense, Dickens could be said to be one of the first celebrity supporters when, as a result of his endorsement, Great Ormond Street Hospital doubled in size from the proceeds of one fundraising event. Delving further into the past, the Society for the Propagation of the Gospel enjoyed the endorsement of a number of post-Reformation monarchs and we can even find biblical precedent for high-profile appeals in Paul's Letters to the Corinthians.

But what has changed is the proliferation of both charities and personalities in the twenty-first century. So are there enough to go round and if so, what do we mean by 'personalities'?

What do we mean by 'personalities'?

It is fair to assume that we all have a reasonably firm understanding of what constitutes a 'charity' although even that is periodically subject to government review, but the meaning of the term 'personality' as used for the purposes of this book needs a little clarification.

Our trusty *Concise Oxford Dictionary* defines personalities as 'individuals who, by virtue of their character, background and general demeanour, are considered to be interesting and/or popular'.

For our present purposes, we should also add the words: 'by the public at large or by a significant, clearly defined section of the population.' After all, by the dictionary definition, my local butcher is a personality but, worthy fellow as he is, his signature is unlikely to feature in anyone's autograph book. This is because my local butcher is not famous – other than among his very happy customers and with his friends down at the pub. It was the late Alan Coren who observed that 'being a personality is not the same as having one'. The reverse is also true: 'having a personality is not the same as being one.'

Personalities may be engaged in many and various fields of human endeavour – from the most obvious worlds of entertainment, music, sport or the media to ostensibly less glamorous spheres such as medicine, religion, commerce or education. The important common factor from the point of view of charities is that they are all 'high profile' either nationally or within a particular field or specific sector of the community. They have a voice to which people will listen, and in many cases they are in a position to act as role models and to set examples which people wish to follow.

Having said all this, it is important to keep a sense of perspective. The beneficial effects of high-profile charity involvement can be realised only if there is a proper match between charity and celebrity. While it is true to say that all patrons and presidents will be personalities, not all personalities will be suitable patrons or presidents for your charity. Indeed, some personalities may be unsuited to fly the flag for any charitable cause. This could be for a number of reasons: they may have achieved fame through notoriety in one way or another; they may not have the particular abilities to represent the charity or front public events or they may be a 'seven-day wonder' as a result of a brief appearance on TV. We all know of celebrities who are 'famous for being famous' but for no other discernible reason.

Speaking of 'celebrities' . . .

Celebrities – who needs them?

Let's clear up what we mean here by 'celebrities'. The correct meaning of the term is simply a person who is celebrated for doing something worthy of admiration. Thus, the terms 'celebrity' and 'personality' could be seen as virtually synonymous. However, in its modern usage, the word is frequently used to mean a person whose face and name are well known for any reason – but probably most of all because we've seen them on the telly.

This is not in any way to disparage those who have made a career in that or in any other medium and whose abilities, skills and expertise have made an impression on the public. There are, as we all know, many gifted professionals in the media who, as skilled actors, entertainers or communicators have rightly earned public acclaim. Such individuals come into the category of personalities as defined above and among their ranks can be found many potential patrons, presidents, ambassadors and suchlike.

It is important, though, to be clear about the use of the term 'celebrity' as one of the several categories of personality and to be careful when applying it to particular individuals. For instance, Marshall of the Royal Air Force Sir Michael Beetham, GCB, CBE, DFC, AFC, one of the vice-presidents of the Royal Air Force Benevolent Fund, is a personality within the terms of reference of this book but may not react favourably if referred to as 'a celebrity'!

What are the special factors associated with celebrity involvement that can make it attractive to charities? A spokesman for the Charity Commission suggests that 'using a celebrity will immediately help raise awareness of a charity and help them get mentioned in places where they otherwise wouldn't be. They give access to areas that the charity might not easily find its way into otherwise'. This could, of course, equally apply to other categories of personality but possibly the main quality that celebrities bring to charities is their fame.

Comic Relief has been highly successful in using famous celebrities to entertain the public while conveying serious and important messages. Children in Need, Sport Relief and Live Aid all employ similar techniques to great advantage.

While most celebrities appreciate that their perceived support of a popular charitable cause can result in benefits to their own careers as well as to the charity, the degree of active participation that they are willing or able to provide differs widely. There are those who, while they are happy for their name to be used by a number of charities, are, for a variety of reasons, unwilling to attend functions or events.

In the interests of fairness and to give a totally balanced view, it is also true to say that some celebrities are very happy to get involved with a charity at the coalface, meeting beneficiaries and their families, arranging special days out and providing moral support to staff, with no wish for press coverage let alone public acclaim – anonymous save for the few people for whom they can make the occasion memorable.

Some may prefer to devote a specific amount of their time and/or financial support to perhaps just one charitable cause about which they feel strongly or with which they have a personal link. Harry Potter author, J K Rowling, for instance, supports single mums' charities because she is herself a single mother. Similarly, other celebrities support a particular charity because they were instrumental in founding it – Esther Rantzen with Childline and Lenny Henry with Comic Relief are just two examples.

There can be no doubt that celebrity endorsement can make a real difference to a charity in terms of media coverage and the resulting increase in public awareness. However, there is a belief on the part of a few charities, especially smaller or recently formed organisations, that if they succeed in getting a celebrity, in other words a famous face, on board, their problems will be solved – the public will become aware of their cause and the money will roll in. This is, of course, a dangerous and misguided attitude.

As will be seen later, the first steps towards recruiting high-level patronage or support must include careful research and consideration of why such support is needed and who would be best placed to provide it. This is particularly important when seeking to enlist the services of a celebrity.

One can think of many examples of charities that have benefited greatly from the involvement of stars of film and television. Celebrities have very successfully raised public awareness of a cause and people have followed their example to the advantage of the charity and its work – indeed a number of instances appear in this book. However, there are other cases where charities have had their fingers badly burned simply as a result of failing to do their research. They did not consider whether the celebrity concerned had the appropriate gravitas, permanent status and public persona to represent the charity and advance its cause in the public eye.

Celebrities should be looked at as one category under the general heading of personalities and, as with all the other categories, should be approached only if they are right for your charity. Indeed there are some charities for which celebrity involvement would make no difference, and certain situations where it would be wholly undesirable.

Before getting involved with celebrities, ask yourself the following:

- Do you need celebrity endorsement at all?
- Will celebrity involvement enhance your fundraising?
- Do you know what kind of celebrity you want?
- Is the celebrity sympathetic to your cause?
- Do they appeal to your target audience?

If the answer to each of the above questions is 'yes', then follow the principles involved in the use of personalities generally.

The great and the good

While holidaying in Southern Italy the following inscription on a plaque outside an ancient chapel struck a chord with this particular fundraiser:

The aristocratic customs of ecclesiastic or religius [sic] institutions in Amalfi represented a peculiar aspect of that merchant class nobility who, by way of such pious actions, predictably wished to gain in market speculation while redeeming their own souls at one and the same time.

This is, perhaps, a slightly cynical view of the wealthy and aristocratic families who contributed handsomely to the building and refurbishment of so many beautiful religious buildings at that time. However, it does serve as an example of the important charitable role played by the wealthy and the influential throughout the centuries. The wording of the above plaque emphasises the self-interest factor in the donations made in that particular case but, as fundraisers, we are aware that pure philanthropy is rare. To a greater or lesser degree, most donors expect something in return for their generosity – whether that takes the form of thanks, public approbation, recognition, as in a roll of honour, or, quite simply, the personal satisfaction of knowing that they have made a contribution towards something worthwhile. After all, there is no reason why self-interest cannot exist side by side with a genuine desire to do good.

The charitable role of people who possess wealth, influence and power ('the great and the good') has been of immense importance since ancient times. What has changed is the form that the charitable contributions take, and the public's perception of the contributors.

In the nineteenth century, the squire of the manor, as well as inviting the local peasantry to the big house at Christmas for mince pies and mulled wine would, in many cases, listen to their problems and do what he could to ease their situation by, for instance, refurbishing tied housing or resolving disputes. Landed or titled families would use their influence and wealth to improve social conditions and relieve poverty.

It is important for us to understand why these powerful figures behaved in this way. Was it out of pity? Was it because of their deeply felt wish to help those less fortunate than themselves? There is no doubt that their generosity was, in the main prompted by something which is now largely misunderstood in modern society – *noblesse oblige* – the concept that privilege entails responsibility. The squire of the manor was conscious of his responsibility to his tenants and farm workers; the aristocracy felt it was incumbent upon them to do what they could to use their power and influence to ease the lot of the poor. Of course, not all privileged people fully accepted the burden of this responsibility, but the responsibility was, nevertheless, acknowledged and was the principal motivating force behind the significant charitable contribution of the great and the good.

The good news for us is that the principle of *noblesse oblige* still lives on – though those to whom it could be said to apply carry out their responsibilities in different ways. Look at the websites of charities both local and national and we find numerous examples of the great and the good lending their names as patrons and presidents, chairing regional committees, heading campaigns to save local schools, fronting initiatives to right social wrongs and so on. The contribution of the wealthy and powerful to charitable endeavour is still of immense importance. To overlook this is to ignore a major source of the help we need if we are to succeed in our charities' objectives.

The Royal Family

Noblesse oblige is perhaps nowhere better exemplified than by the significant involvement of members of the Royal Family with charitable causes and the very real difference this can make. As the government website rightly observes: 'having a royal patron provides vital publicity for the work of charities and allows their enormous achievements and contributions to society to be recognised'. The celebrity status of the monarchy dates back more than ten centuries – not many footballers around then!

There are over three thousand organisations that list a member of the Royal Family as their patron or president, covering every area of the charity sector. The Queen is patron of over 600 charities and the Duke of Edinburgh of over 700. Their support is by no means limited to allowing their names to appear on letterheads; they make visits to meet volunteers and beneficiaries, provide support for fundraising initiatives and endorse appeals to potential donors. Their commitment is unquestionable, as is their reliability: the Queen has had to cancel only five appointments in the last twenty years.

Some members of the Royal Family have established their own charities with which they remain closely involved. The Duke of Edinburgh's Award, personally developed by Prince Philip to provide experiences and skills for young people, is an obvious example.

The Prince of Wales is patron or president of more than 400 organisations including his presidency of the 16 charities that he founded personally, of which the most well known is The Prince's Trust, designed to help young people realise their potential. He takes on patronages and presidencies of charities where he can make a real difference by becoming involved and working closely with the organisation.

The Princess Royal takes a very hands-on role as president of Save the Children, Riding for the Disabled and The Princess Royal Trust for Carers, in addition to the many other causes with which she is associated.

There is no official written definition of the roles of patron or president in relation to members of the Royal Family. However, individual charities will have their own established roles and expectations of patrons and presidents. These should be made clear when inviting a member of the Royal Family to take on a role.

A small word of caution here: while, clearly, the appointment of a royal patron or president can carry great benefits to almost any charity, when considering this for your own organisation, bear in mind the difficulties of planning succession while they are still involved.

It is also as well to take into account the lead-time when inviting members of the Royal Family to attend charity events. Planning sessions are usually held twice-yearly to agree the diary for the following six months. Depending where in that sequence your event comes, this could result in a certain feeling of panic if there is little time between receiving the OK and the date of the event. Alternatively, if your event is towards the latter part of the period under consideration, then you will have time to plan the details after the invitation has been accepted.

Other categories of personality

Personalities can be usefully grouped into categories for the purpose of determining their appropriateness for leading roles in charities. As well as the great and the good and the Royal Family there are many other categories equally worthy of consideration. These include:

- **Politics** – Prominent members of the government of the day or of the opposition are recognised by the public. They clearly occupy positions of power and influence, which may properly be used to highlight a cause that is considered to be in the public interest. Occupants of the backbenches, although sometimes less widely known, can also be of great help, particularly in local matters affecting their constituents.

- **Religion** – High-ranking clergy of all faiths carry a voice which is listened to by their adherents and, in the right cause, can be influential in getting a message across to those of their faith. In addition, many local religious leaders play an active part in the affairs of charities serving their areas.

- **Commerce** – Entrepreneurs and businessmen frequently have leading roles in companies, which take into account the principles of corporate social responsibility.

- **Education** – Leading figures in the world of education, be they head teachers, members of boards of governors or, indeed, Cabinet ministers, can prove willing and able advocates for matters relevant to their calling – again, on either a national or local basis.
- **Health** – Eminent surgeons or physicians, medical scientists and others in this field are well placed to lend influential support to relevant causes; notably health, medical research and environment charities.
- **Entertainment and the media** – We have already looked in some detail at celebrities but the media (for which purposes we include the press, television and radio) employ a wide range of people, some of whom are in positions of considerable power – editors, producers, channel bosses. Many have names (if not always faces) that are known to the public and their positions can open doors and help to bring charities into a greater sphere of awareness.
- **Sport** – Leading figures in the world of sport are very attractive to charities. Sports people are frequently recognised and admired by large sections of the public, so their sphere of influence can extend beyond their own sport and their views on a variety of topics can carry weight with their followers.

The above list is by no means exhaustive and a little research will usually throw up the names of personalities in any number of widely disparate fields. As always, be creative! Look around and you will certainly find a leading figure in an area of activity relevant to your charity.

Who's using whom?

Personalities are, by definition, leading figures in their field and, indeed, it is that quality which makes them attractive to charities. However, becoming involved with a leading figure carries with it attendant problems. Leaders are used to leading – be certain they are leading in the right direction for you.

Agents will wish to ensure that their famous clients are being seen with the right causes. While the celebrity can raise the profile of the charity, the charity can provide the caring face that the celebrity is eager to display. The symbiotic relationship that exists between charity and personality must be mutually satisfying if it is to produce benefit, and such benefit must be to both parties if it is to be sustainable.

PR guru Max Clifford is regularly approached by charities who wish to get close to his clients. He also approaches charities on behalf of clients who ask for his advice upon their possible involvement with charities. As he explained when I met him: 'the UK media are amongst the most savage in the world and anything that genuinely shows celebrities in a good light has to be good for them as well as the charity concerned'.

Having said that, it must be remembered that charities exist to advance the cause envisaged by their founders, not to further the careers of celebrities. Certainly, personalities are entitled to expect to derive benefit from their charitable activities and to enjoy a warm relationship with the charity concerned, but the charity must never 'take its eye off the ball' and be led into a situation in which the personality begins to take control of the game. The charity itself must be presumed to know best what will work for the good of its beneficiaries and must therefore have control of its activities, allocating relevant tasks to its willing volunteers and ensuring that those volunteers are treated with proper respect in the process.

The link between charities and personalities is of very significant importance to charities and personalities alike. But it is the charities alone who have the responsibility of ensuring that this link is used to the maximum advantage of their beneficiaries. That responsibility cannot be taken lightly.

Checklist for Personalities

- Personalities can set an example that people can follow
- Personalities may be high profile but not internationally famous
- All patrons and presidents will be personalities
- Not all personalities make suitable patrons or presidents
- Personalities help raise awareness and 'open doors'
- For some charities celebrity involvement would make no difference
- Charities must use this relationship responsibly for all concerned.

CASE STUDY

MERU and Laurence Llewelyn-Bowen

The Medical Engineering Resource Unit (MERU) improves the lives of children and young people with severe disabilities by using design and engineering skills to make individual pieces of specialist equipment. The charity came into being through the combined efforts of Mr William Bond, a senior lecturer in engineering design, and Mr Trefor Llewellyn Bowen, a consultant orthopaedic surgeon, who was also the father of internationally known interior designer, Laurence Llewelyn-Bowen.

Susan Brumpton, MERU's chief executive, explains just how important this family connection has been for MERU, more than 30 years since it was founded. 'MERU has always been proud of the fact that we were founded by Trefor Llewellyn Bowen, along with Bill Bond, but we had never dared to approach Laurence to act as our patron. We were aware that he is a very busy person who actively supports a lot of charities, so we weren't sure what his response would be. But we eventually got up the nerve to ask and were delighted by his enthusiastic "yes"!

'Laurence has a fantastic group of people behind him, headed up by his wife Jackie and including their two daughters, so it's actually like having a whole team of patrons in one! When they all came to our open day, Laurence made a point of saying how pleased he felt at being able to use his own profile to bring visibility to the work of the charity his father founded. We really appreciate this too, and are looking forward to working with him to our mutual benefit.'

The charity adopted a step-by-step approach in seeking Laurence's support, as marketing and communications manager, Sue Burch, explains. 'We originally asked Laurence if he would agree to be photographed with our "Bugzi", a powered wheelchair for toddlers, and to make a comment about its design. This was for a leaflet promoting the benefits of powered mobility for very young disabled children. He was happy to do this and we got a great photo and a quote, which we have used in subsequent promotion for Bugzi.

'Through emails and phone calls I built up a good relationship with the lady who was Laurence's PA at the time. I felt confident that I could sound her out on his likely reaction if we asked him to be our patron, so I emailed her. When she replied that he would be delighted, the chairman of our trustees wrote and asked him formally. Laurence wrote a lovely letter back, accepting the role and reminiscing about visiting MERU with his father.

'We arranged a meeting between our chief executive, Laurence's wife Jackie and myself, to discuss how they might like to be involved. Jackie offered us the opportunity to appear in their Living TV programme *To The Manor Bowen*, so we arranged our July Open Day around their schedule. The TV crew filmed them visiting us and the programme was shown with a great segment on MERU. We are now hoping to work on various other ideas. Laurence and Jackie are very busy people, so we don't want to bother them too much, but I am in regular contact with both their PAs, who are extremely kind and helpful.'

And how does Laurence himself feel about being involved with MERU? 'Whilst the family link is of course very strong, it is also really important that the work of the charity interests me personally – it is very practical, with straightforward goals and it's easy to see the difference MERU makes. It is the couture of disability charities. It was my father's medical and engineering skills which created the charity and now it's up to me to use my profile to develop it further.'

3

Their roles within your organisation

- Why do you want them to help?
- What do you want them to do?
- Celebrities adding value

Why do you want them to help?

Before launching an initiative to attract high-level personalities to your cause, whether to be patron, president or indeed to fill any other role, first give a thought as to why you want them. Examine the progress the charity is already making right across its work and decide whether or not the additional involvement of a personality or two could enhance that development.

Could it really make a significant difference, for example, to your fund-raising activities? Would you attract additional supporters if you were able to invite them to events where they could mingle with the glitterati? Or are your supporters not, in the main, the sort of people who would be influenced one way or the other by such opportunities? There is little point in working furiously for many months to put on a rock concert by a super-star if you can't sell the tickets.

On the other hand, if your charity's work includes a campaigning element, could your message be put across more effectively and to a wider audience if conveyed by a popular figure whose example people may wish to follow? Have you tried unsuccessfully to bring your cause to the attention of those in authority whose help is needed to effect change, whether by legislation or public opinion? Perhaps a sympathetic leading figure could open the door to the corridors of power wherein lies your help. Will it be important for them to be able to speak about your cause with authority and from a background of personal experience? This might limit your choice but nevertheless would give credibility to the message.

Do you need to attract the interest of the media in order to raise your profile? If so, should you go ahead at whatever cost to your reputation, and most importantly, to your direction? Why not begin by taking a good look at your mission statement, vision and values – concepts so beloved of management consultants, but nevertheless a very important guide to determining what your charity is about and where it should be going. Before you begin to consider who you want, make quite sure that the involvement of a high-level leading figure can be accommodated within the overall strategy of the organisation and, most importantly, can 'add value' to the cause.

You will also need to give attention to the way in which the involvement of a high-profile leading figure will impact upon your existing volunteer base. Will the chairman of the trustees – and, indeed, the members of the board – be comfortable becoming linked with and working with a particular personality? Or is there a danger that they may feel that their contribution to the charity – perhaps over many years – is being devalued by your expressed desire to 'get somebody famous and important on board'?

One way of minimising any resistance or anxiety from the trustees is the idea of recruiting a personality to come from the trustees themselves. Though this can bring its own problems – since the ideas as to which particular figures should be targeted might range from the fanciful to the downright wholly unsuitable, possibly influenced by celebrity X who 'has done marvellous things for my friend's charity'. In such cases, it is your role to move them gently on from fantasy to reality without loss of self-respect – possibly by suggesting alternatives or by explaining that this may not be the optimum time to seek high-level support at all; better to wait until the staffing position is a little more settled or the decisions regarding the capital appeal are finalised . . . or the pigs are harnessed and ready to take off.

As we have seen, the potential benefits of association with the right high-profile figures can be of tremendous value to almost any charity at the right time and in the right circumstances. To ignore the possibilities for your organisation is to overlook an important source of help. However, it is very important that any move in that direction is preceded by careful consideration of the reasons for wanting such involvement and the desired outcome for your cause. Only when everyone concerned is in agreement on these points can discussions proceed to the next stage, namely the question of how best to utilise the services of a personality.

What do you want them to do?

The ways in which personalities can help charities are as many and varied as the innovative ideas of the fundraisers. The form which that help takes is dependent partly upon the degree of involvement the personality is prepared to contribute, but also upon the area of the charity's work which would gain most from the association and the tasks that will produce the most benefit to the cause.

As to the degree of involvement, this can range from the very occasional use of a name right up to active, personal involvement in the work of the charity, but to be effective, the role of patron or president should at the very least include the use of their name on the charity's literature and personal attendance at one or two milestone events in each year.

Other roles, such as vice-president, ambassador and other patrons can be tailor-made to suit the charity's needs, having regard to the particular qualities and attributes of the personality concerned. Importantly, appointments to such roles can be for a specific period and for a defined purpose within one aspect of the charity's work. This avoids the premature commitment to an ongoing relationship and can be very effective in generating interest as well as giving credibility for a specific campaign.

Below is a more detailed look at those tasks that could benefit various aspects of a charity's activities.

Public relations

- The use of the personality's name and/or photograph on general literature and publicity material – This increases the public's association of the charity with the personality and, if the 'fit' is right, contributes greatly to the public image of the organisation.
- Being interviewed in the media – In such cases it is essential to bear in mind the importance of proper briefing. A well-informed public figure can, given a media platform, increase the public's understanding of and

sympathy with the charity very significantly. However, a badly briefed and ill-informed message to the media can be positively harmful and any resultant misconceptions on the part of the public can be very difficult to rectify.

Celebrities in particular are great for getting media coverage but this alone does not necessarily lead to a major increase in fundraising income. Keep your fundraising 'ask' firmly embedded in your PR campaign and make sure your celebrities are aware of it too. In particular, make sure that any magazine articles that mention their involvement with your charity include contact details of the charity, thus making it easy for the reader to respond positively if their interest and support have been aroused. It is surprising how often this can be overlooked.

Fundraising

- The personality's signature on funding applications – This can increase the impact of appeals by a considerable factor. Frequently the public feels a personal acquaintance with the familiar faces seen on television or in the newspapers, and a request that comes from a known source is far more attractive than an impersonal appeal from people we've never heard of – no matter how urgent and important the cause.
- Attracting sponsorship – The higher the profile of the event, the more likely it is to attract sponsorship from companies that recognise the publicity opportunities and the chance to invite important customers to join them at the event.

Campaigning

- Endorsement of specific campaigns – The association of a well-known figure with a charity's message can not only increase its audience but also prove a persuasive factor in influencing people to agree with it.
- Representing the interests of the charity to third parties – Important messages need to reach the ears of those who are in a position to act upon them in a positive and practical way.
- Press coverage – Writing press releases that end up appearing in the local paper may be exactly what you need if yours is a purely local cause but if your intended audience is wider, then a personality may be able to open the right doors with the national press.

- Petitions – These can be of use in demonstrating the extent and depth of public feeling in relation to a particular issue but their effectiveness obviously depends upon as many people as possible signing them. A personality's signature can help drum up the support you need.

- Making speeches – A personality who is well versed in the art of public speaking can make a big impression on an audience. Here again, the importance of thorough briefing cannot be stressed too highly. Speeches are often followed by questions from the floor and this will always show up an inadequate knowledge or understanding of the charity.

The work of the charity

- Visiting a project – This can be of great value in motivating and inspiring operations staff and volunteers, to whom a personal visit from a personality displaying genuine interest in their work can be a source of great encouragement.

- Meeting beneficiaries and their families – This can be particularly uplifting when the personality concerned has personal experience of the problems or disadvantages suffered by the beneficiaries.

Celebrities adding value

While all personalities (as the term is being used here) are well known either to the general public or to a section of the population, all celebrities are, by definition, known to the great majority of people across the UK and possibly beyond. In addition, their fame is often independent of the reason for which they were originally brought to the public's attention. They are, in short, famous people and will continue to be so until the public tires of them. This, in itself, can add to their value as far as charities are concerned.

Whereas the skills and abilities of politicians, sportsmen, eminent scientists and the like are obvious and clearly defined, those of celebrities cover a wide range of activities, as do their talents and personal attributes – from effective verbal communication to musical ability, from cooking to comedy and from publicity to partying. But it is their fame which is of particular interest to charities when considering their usefulness in filling certain roles.

There are a number of tasks that, because of a need to generate wide public attention, are particularly suitable for celebrities as opposed to other categories of personality. These could include:

- Generating or facilitating general media coverage for the charity – Many celebrities, frequently via their publicity agents, have channels of communication with the press, television and radio that can be used effectively to produce otherwise unobtainable coverage of the charity's work.
- Signed photographs or memorabilia for auction or raffle prizes are always in demand – There are countless examples of commonplace items of clothing, for instance, that have been worn by celebrities, fetching quite startling prices, whether at charity auctions or on eBay. Would that my husband's socks carried a similar value!
- Hosting or attending fundraising events – The desire to meet in person those whose names and faces are familiar to us is strong, whether from curiosity, affection, antipathy or the possibility of recounting the experience to our friends. This makes attendance at events where such meetings are possible an attractive proposition.
- Appearances or voice-overs on videos, DVDs etc. – The appeal of a well-known face or voice presenting your charity's case on a well-made video or DVD is obvious. There is also the advantage that those celebrities who are professionals in the field of communication are likely to deliver a presentation of a high quality.

The above is, by no means, an exhaustive list of the ways in which charities can make use of the fame and, in some cases, the personal aptitudes and accomplishments of celebrities, and many organisations are to be applauded for their creativity in this respect. Your own charity will have its own particular order of priorities from the list of tasks but whatever you decide are the most important for you, it is essential that the nature and extent of your expectations are explained in detail to your chosen personality right from the start. Discuss with them just how they would like to be involved; then there is a chance you will actually get a 'round peg for a round hole'.

Pamela Gregory, fundraising and media communications manager of Age Concern, Surrey says that the charity makes full use of celebrities to 'open doors, provide contacts, give appropriate quotes, raise profile, give their name to an appeal, participate in fundraising events and give after-dinner speeches'.

- The annual ball held by the British Red Cross recently raised over £400,000, benefiting from the attendance of several celebrities including Kimberley Walsh and Cheryl Cole of the pop group Girls Aloud, and actress Joan Collins.
- Actor Johnny Depp and football star David Beckham were among those who contributed to *Celebrity Handprints*, a book published in aid of Children in Need and Great Ormond Street Hospital.
- Comedian Ronnie Corbett gave a stand-up performance at a show in Hertford, raising £7,000 for HFT (formerly the Home Farm Trust).
- Pop band McFly are encouraging children to sign up to Pups Club, the junior supporters club of the Guide Dogs for the Blind Association.

These and countless other examples illustrate how charities benefit from associations with celebrities and are a credit to both the organisations and the celebrities concerned. Consider all the forthcoming activities or events planned across all departments and branches of your charity. Is the event you need them for appropriate, or should you choose another? Be creative and look at ways of involving them which links with something they are presently promoting or are interested in.

Checklist for their roles within your organisation

- Consider the roles you wish personalities to play before approaching them
- Will they need to speak about your cause with authority?
- Do they need to have had relevant personal experience?
- Is what you are asking them to do appropriate for them?
- Celebrities attract media attention but not necessarily increased income unless you ask for it.

CASE STUDY

Breakthrough Breast Cancer

Tanya Winch, celebrity and PR manager at Breakthrough Breast Cancer, says that the involvement of celebrities makes a major difference to the charity and is a significant factor in opening doors where appropriate. She feels that by working with celebrities who fit with Breakthrough's brand values it enables the celebrity and PR team to market Breakthrough's fundraising, campaigning and education work more effectively.

The charity benefits from the ongoing active support of its Royal patron, HRH The Prince of Wales, who commits to one appearance a year and has helped Breakthrough achieve national recognition for its work and for its vision of a future free from the fear of breast cancer. Jeremy Hughes, chief executive, liaises with Clarence House and decides which activity is the most appropriate use of HRH's time each year.

Other patrons are appointed to help with specific campaigns or events, each appointment being initially for a period of one year to give the charity and the celebrity a chance to evaluate their involvement before committing to further support. Frequently this leads to long-term relationships – Gaby Roslin has been patron of Breakthrough's flagship fundraising campaign, The £1,000 Challenge, for a number of years and Joseph Fiennes is a member of the Breakthrough Generations Appeal Board after having had a family experience of breast cancer.

In addition to this, Tanya recruits a 'face' or several 'faces' each year to front Fashion Targets Breast Cancer, a national fashion campaign which raises money for Breakthrough through the sale of T-shirts and other fashion merchandise. Past faces have included Sophie Dahl, Jerry Hall, Yasmin le Bon, Twiggy Lawson, Claudia Schiffer and Lily Cole. The 'face' helps promote the campaign by giving Breakthrough one or two days of their time to take part in a photo shoot for the national advertising campaign, and at least one media interview.

The majority of the personalities associated with Breakthrough have a personal connection to breast cancer. How the charity involves them is determined by their skills, experience and availability, and most importantly by what they personally want to do. Working closely with the celebrities and their agents, Tanya waits to see what will fit in with their busy schedules and how best to use them in an ad hoc way before the relationship is developed into a more specific role over time.

Tanya is always on the lookout for additional celebrity supporters and keeps a close ear and eye on the news and media. When a celebrity or relative of a celebrity is diagnosed with breast cancer, Tanya consults with breast cancer experts at Breakthrough to determine the appropriate time and means to approach that celebrity to ask them to support Breakthrough.

4

Who would be good for you?

- Think about your audience
- Getting the right match
- Positioning your cause
- Local causes

Think about your audience

We already know that personalities can be of assistance to us in reaching and communicating with our audience but it is important, for the purpose of deciding which personalities are best suited to the task, to consider very carefully what is meant by our 'audience'. From a fundraising perspective, we are interested mainly in potential donors. However, when considering the involvement of personalities, we must widen our perspective to include in our audience not only those who contribute financially but also those whose attention to the work of the charity may help its development in other ways. Viewed like this, the audience of your charity may be very much wider than you think!

A small disability charity with which I was involved for a number of years gave considerable thought to its wider audience. The guest list for its annual open day provides an excellent example of the diversity of groups which, in the charity's view, made up its audience. These categories included:

- Family and friends of residents, and students, who were thus provided with an opportunity to take part in the activities their relatives were enjoying, and to experience the environment in which they were carried out.

- Health care and social work professionals who were responsible for referring residents, and trainees, who could thereby gain a better understanding of what was on offer and have greater confidence in making future referrals..

- Local residents who, by increasing their understanding, were encouraged to befriend residents whom they met in the local community.

- Local councillors responsible for making decisions regarding planning applications and local services affecting the ongoing life of the centre.

- Existing and previous funders. Whether individual donors or representatives of statutory bodies, trusts, local companies and community organisations, they welcomed the chance to see what their contributions had made possible.

- Prospective funders, for whom this proved a valuable way to increase their understanding of the charity's work, so improving the chances of success for future approaches.

- Potential volunteers from among local residents and company employees who, through meeting existing volunteers, were encouraged to offer their own services in providing the practical help which was so essential for the life of the centre.

- Prospective patrons and trustees who were able to gain first-hand knowledge and understanding of the importance of the charity's work.

Attendance on the day itself was regarded as a 'three-line whip' by all staff and volunteers and it was usual for the president – a representative of the local 'great and good' – to attend together with any celebrities who could be persuaded to put in an appearance. The presence of such personalities attracted those who were unfamiliar with the centre. It also greatly encouraged the residents and their families, who were made to feel 'special', and the staff and volunteers, who gained inspiration and motivation from knowing that their dedicated work had not passed unnoticed by the wider community.

You will already have thought carefully about your audience in terms of your general fundraising strategy. It is important also to look at your audience in the wider context of those whose awareness and empathy can make a significant difference to the furtherance of your cause.

Not all the audience categories listed in the example above will be relevant for your charity but there will certainly be others that are important for your particular cause. After all, your charity is unique.

Getting the right match

In the same way that your charity is unique, so are personalities – each one a separate individual with his or her own skills, character and aspirations and each with his or her own audience. No single personality will appeal to all sections of society and not all charitable causes will appeal to all personalities.

Having established the audience that you want to reach, the next step is to decide what kind of personality is best suited to help you do it. This is largely influenced by your type of cause. A medical research charity, for instance, may well benefit from the credibility arising from association with an eminent scientist whereas an organisation concerned with the homeless may not. A renowned sportsman may provide a popular and persuasive voice for a youth-related cause but an overseas aid agency might gain more from the powerful influence that a politician can bring to bear.

Max Clifford advises: 'it's all about getting the right person for the right audience' and suggests carrying out market research among your own supporters as to whom they would like to see involved.

Celebrities, of course, as a category of personality, have the ability to appeal to a large number of people right across the population. Their fame can sometimes be used as a draw for public events and functions irrespective of the nature of your cause. But here again, it is important to recognise that one charity's ideal celebrity is another's anathema. What works for one will not necessarily do so for another. And don't be influenced by your own personal likes and dislikes. We all have our favourite celebrities and also our pet hates, but remember that it is not you who needs to be attracted by the personality – it is your charity's audience.

Just as the personality must be right for the charity, so the charity must be right for the personality. Is what you are doing within the experience and expertise of the personality? Is it likely to appeal to him or her in a personal capacity? Research the interests and activities of the personality; check on their background – what causes they have supported in the past and any events in their own lives that may make your charity attractive to them.

Also pay attention to any factors associated with them, which may conflict with the principles and ethos of your organisation.

Breakthrough has a number of corporate relationships, which sometimes recruit their own personalities for particular events, but there must still be an appropriate match between the personality and the Breakthrough brand, irrespective of the relationship the company may have with them.

As we've seen, achieving the right match is vital if the association is to enhance external perception of the charity's work. Nonetheless, if we view the coming together of charity and personality as a marriage, it is also vital for the effectiveness and sustainability of the relationship that the chemistry between the two is based on mutual respect. Personalities also have personalities; and some may by nature be very outgoing and used to making their presence felt, which is after all part of their job, whether they are leading professional figures, politicians, sportsmen or stars of reality TV shows. This is one of the main reasons charities value their help in reaching out to their audiences and making an impression. However, this quality also has implications within the organisation itself.

Your charity may already have a patron and/or president as well as other volunteers. It will certainly have trustees and staff, all of whom may need to work with any new personality introduced into the mix. Be sensitive to the dynamics of the situation – the last thing you want is to gain a personality but lose the trust of your loyal and faithful team! As always, careful and diplomatic management can be the key.

There again, you may already benefit from the involvement of another personality or personalities. Ensure that any new introduction is compatible with both the charity's brand and the existing high-level associates. A fashion show, for instance, is not improved by famous figures disputing over who should be in charge of the microphone! The way to avoid such potentially calamitous situations is to think very carefully about the mix before you start baking the cake.

Sometimes there might be a personality who is already a major donor to your charity and whom you might consider approaching to seek their involvement as a patron, president or in some other role. In such cases, bear in mind the possibility that their acceptance of such a post may threaten the continuance of their donations. Consider the best use of the personality concerned for both the short- and longer-term benefit of the charity.

Positioning your cause

There are usually around 15 traders selling their wares in my local weekly market and each one needs to set out his stall in the best possible position in order to attract the most custom – some on the edge of the square to catch the attention of passing trade, some at the centre of the throng to attract regular market-goers. Others rely on their ability to shout their wares loudly wherever they are placed.

There are nearly 200,000 registered charities in the UK and each one of them needs to display its wares in the most appropriate site – some in the tabloids, some in the broadsheets, some in the specialist press within their own particular sector. There are charities whose message needs to reach the corridors of governmental power, others who need to capture the attention of the young and still others whose cause is of interest to patrons of the arts or to animal lovers. It's a very large and varied market place and your choice of personality will depend mainly upon your chosen place within it.

Perhaps you need to push your charity's cause up the political agenda, in which case you need to consider the contribution that a Member of Parliament could make – though you need to target those with a personal connection to your cause. They are likely to be interested in the opportunity to bring about real change in a situation, which both motivates them and fits in with their own political persuasion. Interestingly, NCVO (National Council for Voluntary Organisations) runs an MP's Secondment Scheme designed to help charities that find it difficult to attract support from politicians.

Or is your cause of potential interest to the elderly? In organising Age Concern's annual Songs of Praise at Guildford, the team would look for a mature person such as actress Jean Boht to give a reading, who would be an attraction for the congregation attending. But for a black-tie fund-raising dinner they enlist the help of a celebrity such as Max Clifford or Chris Tarrant who will prove a draw to a younger element, thereby widening their database.

An important point to bear in mind is the need to ensure that your 'vision' is in safe hands. It is easy to overlook the possibility that, by an ill-advised choice of personality, you might run the risk of dumbing down serious concerns to which your charity wishes to draw attention. A circus clown could liven up an event for a children's charity and draw attention to its message but would be wholly inappropriate as a voice for an organisation dealing with abuse of the elderly. This may be an extreme example perhaps, but the same principle applies, to a greater or lesser extent, in any association between charity and personality.

The other side of the coin is that in asking personalities to represent your cause in whatever capacity, you are asking them to do something which may impact upon their own positions in the publicity market place. Like charities, personalities also have a need to appeal to a particular audience and are unlikely to align themselves with a cause which may alienate them from their own fans, followers or friends. Here, then, is another example of why an association between a charity and a personality must be to the benefit of both if it is to be successful.

Local causes

Smaller or locally based charities are sometimes deterred from approaching nationally known figures because they do not believe their cause is sufficiently important to be of interest to anyone outside their locality. This is very much a misguided view. Research shows that many famous or leading figures prefer to forge links with smaller lesser-known causes on the grounds that their association can make a very significant difference, bringing the charity's work to the attention of a wider public. Many famous figures live outside London and are involved in areas of activity related to local causes. Local charities can frequently attract support from celebrities who may be reluctant to become too involved with national charities, which could mean spending time out of their busy schedules travelling to London for photo shoots and launches. They prefer to be involved with a local charity because it is more convenient.

An appeal for a new scout hut may be of considerable interest to an international footballer recently moved to a large house just outside the village. A senior Cabinet minister may have recently made a speech in Parliament highlighting the need for communities to address the problems facing elderly people – just the person to head up your campaign to build a new day centre or expand your outreach programme – he or she may even be the MP for a neighbouring constituency.

Listen to local radio, watch regional TV, look at the VIP guests attending an event at your local town hall. Keep an eye on the local paper to see which celebrities will be appearing at a nearby theatre or sports stadium or perhaps opening a new local supermarket. Could this tie in with an event you are planning at around the same time? Be on the lookout for personalities whose interests could include either your cause itself or a particular type of fundraising event you are planning.

The first charity I worked for, some 30 years ago, was a local independent hospital trust. The founding trustees appreciated the importance of raising the profile of this new initiative within the local community, who would benefit when the hospital was built and whose support was needed in order to achieve it. This might have seemed a daunting task if the trustees had been diffident in trying to attract the interest of personalities who might help them in this endeavour.

Fortunately, a few of the trustees were keen golfers who, through their membership of the local golf club, were able to enlist the support of a number of celebrities of the time – Norman Wisdom, Henry Cooper and Jim Davidson among them – all of whom agreed to take part in a pro-am celebrity golf tournament.

As a result, many local businesses were very happy to sponsor tees, advertise in the brochure and bring guests to the event. The tournament also attracted the interest of the reporter and photographer from the local newspaper who covered the event extensively in the next weekly edition. Success all round – substantial funds were raised, new supporters were recruited and awareness of the charity was increased very significantly among the target audience for the appeal. What's more, the personalities involved were able to enjoy a day doing something they loved.

The lesson to be learned is that, no matter how large or small your charity, no matter whether your cause is local, national or international, it is possible, with a little research, to find a way through to personalities who are, by their association with you, able to help you achieve your goals. All that is needed is the will to find that common factor, which brings together charity and personality in a shared interest and which produces satisfaction to both. If you are good for them, they will be good for you.

Checklist for who would be good for you?

- No personality will appeal to all sections of society
- Look for someone who will appeal to your target audience

- Is what you are asking them to do within their personal experience?
- Do they have the necessary expertise to carry it out?
- Consider how existing patrons would feel about this association
- It is important to identify an appropriate match for the charity brand
- Will your vision be safe or are you dumbing down serious concerns?
- Where do you want to be positioned in the media?
- Some personalities prefer to forge links with lesser known causes.

CASE STUDY

Parkinson's Disease Society

As a charity dedicated to supporting people with Parkinson's, their families, friends and carers, it is important that the patron and president have not only an understanding of this disease when meeting medical professionals but also have the caring and sensitive approach that is so very important when meeting those personally affected. These qualities are present in full measure in both their Royal patron and president.

As patron, HRH The Duchess of Gloucester attends at least one event for the charity every year. This has included a reception in Northern Ireland, bringing together health and social care professionals and local branches of the Society. This event helped to develop links between the Society and local clinical and care services. Her involvement has ranged from visiting the Exeter branch of the Society to attending the annual carol concert in London's Southwark Cathedral.

Jane Asher has been supporting the Society for a number of years, since her brother-in-law has the disease. This has involved her in hosting the London carol concert for a number of years, as well as other fundraising and promotional events. In 2007 she became president and her involvement helps to raise awareness through the media and the events she attends. This is of great benefit in generating funds and she will shortly be fronting her first direct mail appeal for Parkinson's Disease Society.

'Having the active involvement of HRH The Duchess of Gloucester and Jane Asher is extremely important to the PDS. Both are hugely committed to supporting people with Parkinson's, which makes their participation very powerful, and their roles and personal qualities complement each other well,' says Hugo Middlemas, director of fundraising.

5

How to identify and find your potential leaders

- Who's out there?
- How to find them
- Opportunism
- Piggy-backing

Whenever I speak with charities on the subject of leading figures, the question they ask most often is 'how do you find them?' Indeed that was one of the reasons for writing this book. Having considered what is meant by personalities, the appropriate time to enlist their support, the ways in which they could help and who would be best for your charity, the question of finding them is put into perspective.

So where do we start? Look around . . .

Who's out there?

Bearing in mind the importance of finding the right match for your organisation, look first for any high-profile figures who are already speaking out in support of a similar cause but who as yet have no personal involvement with your charity. Perhaps there is a politician whose enthusiasm for a cause linked to yours has been headlined recently? Such a powerful figure with a ready-made knowledge and understanding of your message may be more than willing to demonstrate his or her personal commitment by lending his name to a project or publicly endorsing your work.

Or perhaps you know of a particular celebrity who has personal experience of a disease for whose victims you raise funds. Whether the celebrity has contracted the condition personally or witnessed the suffering of a family member, it is likely that a relationship with your charity will be strong and lasting, arising as it does from a personal and deeply felt desire to help.

Similarly, there may be personalities who have successfully overcome the problems affecting those whom your charity helps, and would be happy to say so publicly to demonstrate their recovery. Most people welcome the opportunity to say thank you – you could give them that opportunity. Frequently also, the desire to 'give something back' is strong among those who have been helped through distressing situations and this can sometimes lead to a strong and lasting hands-on involvement – particularly, perhaps, for charities dealing with issues such as homelessness, unemployment, drug and alcohol addiction or even domestic violence.

Even if a personality has no direct personal experience of the need which your charity addresses, it may be that his or her particular profile would appeal specifically to the audience you wish to reach. An example of this could be a storyline in a popular television soap opera which coincides with your cause, thereby bringing it to the attention of the masses. Given your interest in and experience of the cause, an approach to the actors, writers or producers would be perfectly reasonable and their support could well be forthcoming. Better still, the programme makers may welcome an opportunity to consult you to ensure that their portrayal of the problem is realistic and sensitive. Such an involvement could lead to a useful ongoing relationship with the people concerned, possibly leading to opportunities to open further doors in the media world.

Look also at other charities in a similar field to yours. While one would certainly not advocate 'poaching' personalities from other organisations, it sometimes happens that high-profile figures support a particular cause but have only peripheral involvement with a specific charity or charities. In such cases, they may look favourably on an approach from your organisation for a similar involvement – especially if they feel at home with your team.

How to find them

Although we sometimes regret the fact that, in this age of global media and universal information technology, little can be kept private, for those of us looking for the right names for our charity it means that finding them has never been easier. Consider an average day for many of us. Perhaps our morning ablutions are made to the accompaniment of breakfast television or *Wake up to Wogan*, followed by the daily papers. A walk or drive to the station takes us past advertising hoardings and the placards of newsvendors. During the subsequent ride on the train, bus or tube, we are obliged to sit looking at posters featuring celebrities promoting toothpaste, telephone services or cosmetics – or listening to the sound of the latest hits leaking from the headphones of the passenger next to us. After a hard day at the office, we are pleased to enjoy a ready-made meal endorsed by a celebrity chef. Then we can relax in front of the TV to watch our favourite soap or a chat show in which celebrities open their hearts to the equally celebrated interviewer, followed by the news and, possibly, a current affairs programme. Perhaps half an hour's random googling on the computer follows before we retire to bed – not forgetting to set the radio alarm to our favourite station. Finding and learning about famous names and faces are not a problem – getting away from them can be.

Information about personalities is all around us. Our task is to sift this mountain of data and to narrow down the search for a suitable candidate or candidates for the particular purpose we have in mind. Do any of the famous names and faces we encountered yesterday have anything in common with our cause? Look for clues – what was that politician saying on the news last night about unemployment? Didn't that celebrity on breakfast TV mention something about losing a parent recently to cancer? Wasn't that celebrity chef whose picture appeared on your lasagne package involved in a drive to promote healthy eating? What was that you read in the paper about a famous tennis star wishing to promote more sports facilities for children in deprived areas? Oh and had you realised that the famous rock star who appeared on the pet food advert in the tube was a devoted dog owner? Look for examples of celebrity endorsement of causes aligned to yours.

Obviously, be realistic about the personalities you include on your shortlist. While we must not be diffident about approaching the right person, we must beware of losing our grip on reality. If yours is a small organisation with a low media profile, you are unlikely to attract the attention of an A-list celebrity unless you can establish a firm link either with your cause or with a particular event or project you are planning.

Ask your membership. Do any of them have a connection with a likely candidate for patron or president? Local branches of your charity may already have links with a personality or two – though this will need careful handling, bearing in mind the inevitable territorial nature of regional fund-raising, and may necessitate some horse-trading over how any resulting funds may be allocated. I recall that, many years ago, one of the regional teams of a large national charity had spent many months setting up a charity sports fixture that was attended by a senior member of the Royal Family who was to receive the not inconsiderable cheque which, unfortunately, was taken back to head office and counted as part of the charity's national income. The regional organiser was left feeling somewhat disgruntled at losing the credit for having raised what amounted to his annual target.

Having drawn up your shortlist, there are a number of agencies, listed at the end of this chapter, which provide contact details of personalities – particularly those involved in the entertainment world in its broadest sense.

If you're looking for the great and the good, *Debretts* and *Who's Who* are still probably the best starting point. If it's the wealthiest connections you are trying to make, then there is always the *Sunday Times* Rich List, which can now be searched online – though, of course, you may well be the last in a long line of charities that have already beaten a path to the doors of those who appear in it.

Opportunism

As fundraisers, we are aware of the importance of opportunism – the art of spotting opportunities as they arise and turning them to advantage. And, as we know, this is not something that happens only during 'normal office hours' – we need to be prepared for opportunities to present themselves at any time and, most importantly, to recognise them as such.

I well remember some years ago working for a medical charity that desperately needed to enlist the support of leading figures to enhance its campaigning. The chairman of the charity was extremely well connected and happened to drop into conversation over coffee prior to a trustees' meeting that he was rather tired, having the previous evening been present at a dinner attended by a number of politicians and other personalities. I asked him what interest they had shown in the organisation and was dismayed to be told that he had not got around to mentioning the charity to any of his fellow guests. A sad little tale but it does highlight the importance, not only of being on the lookout for opportunities, but also of recognising them as such and taking advantage of them in any way that presents itself whether we consider ourselves to be 'on duty' at the time or not.

This, of course, entails being thoroughly aware of what is going on in our charities so that we are in a position to make connections and 'press the right buttons' when in conversation with those who may be in a position to help. This applies whether or not the charity is actively seeking a personality for a particular role at the time. If the aforementioned chairman had borne this in mind, he could at least have been able to make some of his influential dinner companions aware of the importance of the charity's work, thus opening the door to keeping in touch with them occasionally, ready for the right time to involve them strategically.

It occasionally happens that an opportunity falls into our lap unbidden, such as when a well-known figure makes contact with a charity instead of the other way round. This is usually motivated by something that the personality has seen, heard or read and that has prompted a desire to help. This happened to the charity Let's Face It when Victoria Wood contacted them after watching a television documentary about facial cancer. She subsequently became the charity's patron. A very successful outcome – though caution is occasionally required. What if the personality in question is wholly unsuitable to be associated with the charity? This could be for a number of reasons – the person may currently be the subject of controversy in the media or perhaps might appeal to an audience which is very far from that which the charity seeks to attract. Saying no in such circumstances can be a delicate and sensitive matter – particularly if there is a risk that the personality may publicise the fact that their generous offer has been spurned. The Institute of Fundraising has a Code of Practice on the Acceptance and Refusal of Donations, which may also be relevant here and which you may care to consult.

To adopt a pragmatic approach to such unwanted offers, it is, in some cases, more likely that the personality has approached you for their own purposes rather than those of your charity. Make clear to them just what would be involved were they to volunteer their services and, in all probability, they will decide for themselves that it would not be in their best interests. This reasonable response to their offer should avoid giving offence and is less likely to result in adverse publicity for the charity.

Remember that a personality's participation in perhaps a single event or function for your charity is in itself an opportunity to pave the way for future involvement on a more lasting basis. Estée Lauder launched Breast Awareness Month some 15 years ago with their Pink Ribbon Campaign. Through careful 'growing on' of the concept, the campaign now provides a significant fundraising opportunity for all the breast cancer charities worldwide – each in its own way. One-third of the fundraising income for Breakthrough comes through activities during Breast Cancer Awareness Month. From little acorns . . .

Piggy-backing

Don't be afraid to link up with other charities that may already have a relationship with someone who could be influential for your charity as well – even for a one-off occasion. Such an arrangement could, if carefully managed, render an event more successful than if you had tried to go it alone. Think laterally about causes which, though not precisely the same as your own, nevertheless have a synergy with your charity and might provide the opportunity you need to attract a new audience. During my tenure as appeals director at The Shaftesbury Society, we shared in a very successful evening with The Orpheus Trust at the time when its founder, Richard Stilgoe, was raising funds to build an inclusive performing arts centre.

Occasionally, such one-off arrangements can lead to longer-term relationships – which brings to mind another example from my time at The Shaftesbury Society involving a joint project in the East End of London with The Griffin Trust and Shaftesbury Housing Association. As a personal friend of the chairman of the Griffin Appeal, HRH The Princess Royal officially opened Lansbury Lodge and several years later, after the death of the Queen Mother, she took over the role of patron of the Shaftesbury Society.

Agencies and other resources

- Equity 0207 379 6000 www.equity.org.uk
- Celebrity Agents 0845 458 3707 www.celebrity-agent.co.uk
- Upfront Celebrity Services 0207 836 7703 www.celebritiesworldwide.com
- The A-List database www.the-alist-org
- The Red Pages www.theredpages.co.uk

- *Spotlight* www.spotlight.com
- *The Stage* www.thestage.co.uk
- Celebrity Database www.celebrityspotlight.co.uk
- *Debretts* 020 8939 2250 www.debretts.co.uk
- *Who's Who* 01256 302699 www.ukwhoswho.com
- Sunday Times Rich List www.timesonline.co.uk/richlist

Useful information sheets

- How do I get celebrity support? www.bbc.co.uk/dna/actionnetwork
- Patrons and celebrity support www.cafamily.org.uk

Checklist for identifying and finding your Personalities

- Who's already out there speaking in support of similar causes?
- Information about personalities is all around us
- A small charity is unlikely to attract an A-list celebrity
- Be prepared for and recognise opportunities that come your way
- Be aware of what is going on in your charity and make the links
- Piggy-backing other charities can bring long-term benefits

CASE STUDY

Dales-Care and Roy Hudd

Dales-Care is a charity based in North Yorkshire, founded in the late 1980s to provide support for elderly people living in the Yorkshire Dales and I became their first executive director. Initially it was planned that Dales-Care would take over a small hospital, shortly to be closed by the local health authority and converted for a wide range of facilities, but until the hospital became available it was difficult to embark upon a major fundraising campaign since we had not actually calculated just how much we needed to raise. However it was important to raise awareness of the needs of the elderly people living in the rather isolated villages spread across the Dales.

While pondering just how to set about illustrating this, without using any real-life examples, I happened to see an episode in the *Talking Heads* series written for the BBC by Alan Bennett. The feelings of loneliness and isolation were perfectly exemplified in the very sensitive portrayal by the late Thora Hird in the episode entitled 'A cream cracker under the settee'. Not knowing either of these very well-known figures, I set about making contact with the BBC and was fortunate enough to capture the imagination of the producer who kindly agreed to let me have a copy of the episode and gave permission for it to be edited down to around ten minutes.

The event which we held to launch the charity was attended by a good number of prospective donors and supporters, and the video put across our message in a way we could not have hoped to achieve in any other way. The quality of Alan Bennett's writing and Thora Hird's performance inspired many to rally to our cause and subsequently to support the appeal.

This was particularly gratifying to me, having gone from working as regional manager in the Midlands for a very large international charity with all the promotional materials one would expect, to leading a very small team – basically of one! Living in a small Yorkshire market town was a new experience for us as a family and we threw ourselves into community life with great enthusiasm –

getting involved in a variety of activities, including their annual Edwardian festival, and this led to another opportunity for Dales-Care.

When I accidentally let it slip that I had been involved in amateur dramatics and musical shows over the years, I was promptly persuaded to produce an old time music hall as part of the festival. Our little troupe of players, though inexperienced, was wildly enthusiastic and in an attempt to focus this enthusiasm I decided that we would all visit the famous Leeds City Varieties Theatre where Roy Hudd was appearing in an old time music hall.

We duly arrived, all bedecked in our Edwardian finery and took our seats near the front of the theatre. Fortuitously, we caught the eye of Roy himself and when he asked all those in the audience who were in costume to stand up, we proudly did so. In response to his enquiry, we said that we would shortly be performing in our own music hall. This gave me yet another idea . . .

In the interval, it was easy to make my way backstage; since as I was in costume the stagehands assumed I was a member of the cast. I found Roy refreshing himself at the bar, and, though slightly surprised to see me, he couldn't have been more charming. In one of my flashes of inspiration, which have frequently been my downfall, I told him that we were putting on the music hall, deciding then and there that it was to be in aid of a local charity, namely Dales-Care, and it would mean so much if he were to wish us well.

He did more than that – he advertised our music hall and the charity in the second half of his show, and subsequently wrote the foreword for the programme. The lift that this gave to both cast and audience was tremendous and all three performances were packed out – even attended by the chairman of the charity who was somewhat taken aback to see his executive director dancing the can-can! But whatever it takes ...

Using my initiative to maximise opportunities such as these for the furtherance of a cause in which I passionately believed, my years at Dales-Care were both a challenge and a joy. Their centre in Bedale bears testimony to the support of such leading figures in its formative years.

6

The approach

- Getting them on board
- The gatekeepers
- The message
- The response

Getting them on board

You've established why your charity needs to involve one or more personalities; you also have a clear idea of what you want them to do; you have decided who would be good for you and you have identified someone you want to approach. So now you are ready for the next stage – how do you get them on board?

Getting people on board. How hard can this be? We're fundraisers, for goodness' sake! It's what we do. But approaching people for cash donations is perhaps rather different to approaching them for their time, their name and their public endorsement of what your charity is all about. As a charity, you are obviously concerned to maintain your good reputation. So are they. This introduces a different element of sensitivity to that which exists in your relationship with a donor, and must be borne in mind throughout all your dealings with high-profile volunteers. You are asking them, in effect, to put their head over the parapet and wave your flag.

Up until now, we've considered the merits of involving personalities from the charity's point of view. However, now is the time to think about things from the personality's viewpoint. Why would anyone step on board your boat unless they have a good reason for doing so?

The research you have already carried out should have thrown up a reason for you to believe that they may be willing to become involved with you, either because of some personal experience or because of the opportunities the relationship would offer. However, the chances are that they are not aware of this perceived link – after all, if they were they would probably be associated with you already in some way. So before you take any steps towards making contact, be very clear as to how you are going to articulate this. Prepare some basic information to make them aware of the work you do and how they would fit into the work of the charity. Explain why you have come to the conclusion that they might have a personal link to the core work of your charity.

Where the reason is based on personal experience, if the information could reasonably be found through newspapers and other media, then you don't need to explain how you know. Indeed, other charities will no doubt also have approached them and if that is the case, you need to set out what is special about you. However if the information about the personality's experience is not widely known, they may not wish it to be – and, furthermore, may take exception to your knowing. In such cases, when approaching them, great care must be taken in raising this subject, and it may well be more sensitive to make an initial contact through a third party who already knows them and is aware of the circumstances.

Be pragmatic about why they may be interested in becoming involved. Whether or not they have a personal connection, celebrities, for instance, may be motivated by the publicity opportunities. This could be a welcome return to the limelight or a way of drawing attention to their current film or book launch. Their support for popular causes is a way of enhancing their public image and it is important to recognise that sincerity and self-promotion can, and frequently do, exist side by side. After all, public figures have a perfectly legitimate responsibility to consider the effect of any charitable involvement on their own careers. An ill-fated association with a charitable cause impacts adversely upon all concerned, not only upon the charity itself.

Many personalities choose one charity, which enables them to focus their support and involvement, and importantly from a practical point of view, enables them to turn away other approaches. They must have their own personal reasons for wanting to be involved and associated with you, and that is what you need to tap into and develop to produce a mutually satisfying relationship. It is important to establish what they expect to get from the role, how they see themselves fitting into the organisation and what personal attributes they feel are most appropriate.

If your charity is involved in medical research or in campaigning to right a social wrong, the personality you have in your sights may be an eminent scientist or politician. In either case, he or she might be looking for an opportunity to attract wider public attention to their work or to a particular movement in society with which they wish to be identified. They would want to be sure that, in helping you, they would be furthering a cause which they believe is important in a way that fits their own approach to the problem.

Bear in mind too that personalities, like donors, are influenced by the involvement of their peers and will want to know which other public figures have a relationship with your charity. They can then make a judgment as to whether being linked with those people through a shared commitment would be helpful or harmful to their own reputations. Others, on the other hand, will prefer exclusivity and would not wish to share the spotlight.

Personalities are no different from anyone else in that committing to an additional undertaking in an already busy life can be difficult, to say the least. They are likely to be apprehensive lest agreeing to one request may lead to others, and so place a greater demand on their time than they are willing or able to satisfy. You have already decided what you want them to do and you know how much of their time this will involve, but they do not. Be clear about this in your initial approach. If, subsequently, other opportunities evolve and it is their wish to develop these, then further discussions can take place at that time.

This need for clarity and truthfulness in making an approach cannot be over-emphasised. Some charities, in an effort to secure the support of a public figure, will say 'we're only asking for your time, not for money' whereas, in reality, their time has a very real monetary value in terms of both working time lost and value to the charity. This is particularly so in the case of personalities whose income is wholly or partially derived from public appearances of one sort or another – be it in the form of lectures, demonstrations, opening fêtes or making after-dinner speeches – for example, in asking a film or television personality to front a promotional video for you, you are asking him or her to make a significant monetary contribution by foregoing the fee that they would receive in other circumstances.

Remember also that your experience of what can go right and what can go wrong in charitable projects is considerably greater than theirs. You have a duty to use your knowledge responsibly in order to manage and direct matters in such a way as to be in the best interests of both your charity and the high-level volunteer you plan to invite on board.

The gatekeepers

We all recognise the importance of carrying out detailed research before embarking on a major gift campaign or developing a direct mail strategy. The process of contacting your chosen personality requires a similar considered and carefully targeted approach.

The scatter-gun approach is not recommended – although, just occasionally, it has been known to work. The Essex-based charity, Action in Mental Health, once sent a generic letter to a whole raft of celebrities asking for memorabilia for an up-and-coming auction. Predictably, most of the responses they received were accompanied by a compliment slip but Hollywood superstar Jackie Chan sent a personal letter sympathising with the aims of the charity and offering to donate substantially to the cause. A reply was sent to him outlining the charity's plans for using the donation and asking whether he would consider linking his name to the charity as patron. He faxed back from Hong Kong agreeing to the request. Quite a result!

However, there are risks involved in this blanket approach method – attracting the wrong personalities for your charity or alienating those whom you would like to have on board, making subsequent approaches less likely to succeed, and so on. Success is more likely using the more targeted approach based on diligent research and careful consideration of the desired outcome. So how do you start?

Cold calling

The most obvious method is a simple cold telephone call to the person concerned, with a view to introducing yourself and your charity. This has two drawbacks. First, there is the practical difficulty of tracking down a telephone number that is likely to be answered by them personally. Most public figures are surrounded in their working environments by a protective barrier of PAs, professional colleagues and advisors, and their private numbers are just that – private.

Second, even if you are successful in tracking them down, such an unsolicited approach is unlikely to succeed. This is not necessarily because they are unsympathetic to you or to your cause but quite simply because the majority of those who are well known and successful in their field are very vulnerable to harassment by all and sundry. Eminent medical practitioners are pestered by those who have a grievance against their profession or who simply want advice without going through the proper channels; leading scientists are approached by amateurs in their field who believe they have hit upon the solution to the riddle of the universe; sporting icons, TV idols and pop stars are besieged by fans; and politicians are buttonholed by almost everyone. Because of this, anyone whose name is well known either nationally or within a particular field, tends to distrust unsolicited direct approaches from strangers – particularly, it must be said, by telephone. They are, after all, by definition, busy people professionally and, in most cases, their private time is precious. When they're able to switch off they don't really want to be switched on.

This is not to say that a direct approach is not worth trying. Indeed, in many ways, personal contact is the very best means of getting your target personality on board. The author Joanna Trollope, for instance, responded to a personal request from a friend of her daughter to speak about the charity The Mulberry Bush to a group of influential women in Oxfordshire. Before carrying out the engagement, she visited the charity and was so impressed with its work that she became a patron. But – and this is a very big but – a telephone call from a total stranger who wishes to persuade you to fit something else into your already bursting schedule is not a personal approach. To someone who is either embroiled in a busy work schedule or snatching a quiet evening with the family, it ranks somewhere in between a sales call from a double glazing company and an anonymous phone call involving heavy breathing. It is an intrusion.

The personal approach

So what is a personal approach? If, while slumped on the sofa, glass of wine in hand, watching your favourite TV show after a long day at the office, you are obliged to get up and answer the telephone only to be met with an unfamiliar voice offering you an unbelievable deal to have your drive re-laid, how do you respond? In those circumstances, even common politeness can be difficult to achieve. If, on the other hand, the caller is an old friend suggesting an evening out to catch up on the latest gossip, your reaction is likely to be very different. The reason is simple – the former is a stranger, the latter is someone with whom you have a personal relationship. Furthermore, if, during the subsequent evening out, your friend mentions that he or she has recently had their drive re-laid and the company gave them a really good deal, you might be tempted to give the firm a call – assuming, that is, you possess a drive and it's in need of attention.

This simple principle must be applied when considering how best to approach your chosen personality. Is there anyone you know who might be personally acquainted with him or her – or with anyone connected with them? If so, that's a good place to start.

The proper channels

If not, then you'll need to proceed through 'the proper channels'. What these channels are will depend very much on who your personality is and what he or she does but, in every case it will involve gaining access to the protective ring of PAs, professional colleagues and advisors referred to above. These are the gatekeepers.

In the case of celebrities such as writers, musicians, TV stars and actors, the most obvious (though not necessarily the best) starting point is the agent. These powerful figures often have the final say in deciding what their client should or should not be associated with, and their sole concern is the impact upon their client's career – that's what they are paid for. If an agent considers that an involvement in your charity would not enhance their client's reputation or image, or would divert him or her from other more profitable activities, it is unlikely that your approach would even be communicated to the client. In fact Max Clifford advises that charities should never approach a celebrity through an agent who will not see this as a priority for their client.

On the other hand, if the agent can see some mileage in the proposed association, then he or she can prove a valuable ally in achieving it. Remember also that agents have staff in their offices who can be useful in finding a way through. They are, if you like, the gatekeepers to the gatekeeper.

An alternative approach to celebrities in this category is via their PAs who frequently have great influence in planning their employer's schedules. The celebrity may agree to participate in, say, an event for you but their PA will know whether or not it can be fitted into the working calendar.

Politicians or their staff can be contacted at the House of Commons, via their surgeries or through their constituency agents or secretaries.

If your target is a leading figure in a profession such as medicine, law or the church, it is likely that your charity already has links with them through your work. Or perhaps one of your trustees has a professional relationship with them?

Leading entrepreneurs can be tricky to reach in that they have a 'protective ring around not just them but their entire organisation, and even if you have an entrée into their company or companies, it is perhaps unlikely (unless you're very lucky) that this will be on a level which would ensure personal access to the 'big boss'. The best course is therefore to research your charity's contacts thoroughly in the hope of finding someone among them who may have a personal connection with the entrepreneur (either as a friend or a fellow club member, for instance) and who might have an opportunity to talk to them either face to face or on the telephone.

Just one word of caution, be very careful about approaching members of the personality's family who may be inundated with requests for introductions to their famous husband/wife/son/daughter/second cousin – not just from friends but also from the press and fans seeking a way through. While, in most cases, they will be proud of the success achieved by their family member, they have their own lives to lead and their own affairs to attend to and should not be expected to act as unofficial gate-keepers. If you are acquainted with a member of your chosen personality's family, then do be sensitive to this and try to avoid intrusion.

To sum up: first, look for a contact or a route through to your chosen personality via someone you already know who may be known to them and therefore is in a position to make a personal approach. If this draws a blank, identify the gatekeepers and make contact, bearing in mind the differing methods of approach required according to their roles within the protective ring. Whoever you approach, be they agent, PA, secretary, colleague or friend, of the Personality you wish to recruit, ensure that they understand fully the objectives of your charity and your reasons for believing that the personality's involvement would help to make a positive and significant difference. If the gatekeeper feels passionately about your cause, the message that ultimately filters through to the personality will be all the more powerful. Unfortunately, there have been cases where some charities have sought to bypass this process altogether – sometimes with undesirable results.

Personalities are, by definition, in the public eye and this glare of publicity frequently extends to their private lives – it goes with the territory. Like anyone else, they experience triumphs and disasters, victories and failures; they make right decisions and bad mistakes; sometimes fate smiles on them and sometimes they suffer misfortune. Unlike the rest of us, however, their actions, both professional and private, are a source of public interest. It has been known for charities to tap into this by exploiting some current wave of public attention, associating the name of a personality with their own because of some perceived link with their work. Where this is done without the prior knowledge or consent of the personality, he or she is unlikely to feel favourably towards the charity and any chance of a formal association at a later date is jeopardised. In addition, the reputation of the charity is endangered.

The message

You've established the route you are going to take and the person or persons who are going to help you along the way but before any steps are taken, you must be absolutely clear as to the message you want to be conveyed to the personality of your choice. At the risk of stating the obvious, it's no use gaining the ear of Santa Claus if you haven't decided what you want for Christmas!

The personality in question may be unaware of the existence of your charity – and if they do know of you, the chances are that they will not be acquainted with how your work is carried out or the extent of the need for it. They therefore need to be provided with information. However, it is essential to avoid overloading them with detail at this early stage. A filing cabinet full of leaflets, annual accounts and reviews, funding analyses and other statistical information will certainly prove counter-productive. All they need at the initial contact is a brief outline of the need your charity is addressing, how you are tackling it and the difference that your input makes.

You will also need to explain why their own particular involvement is so important to you and to the cause, perhaps raising specific points you have learned about them from your research.

In conclusion, you need to explain exactly what it is you want them to do and, initially, it is wise to limit this to something easily achievable and likely to appeal to their enthusiasms and interests. This could be particularly helpful for those newly achieving celebrity status who have yet to decide which causes they wish to support. Providing one-off help to a number of charities will help them to grow whichever relationship feels most comfortable. If they know they could be helping a valuable cause with comparatively little effort on their part, they are more likely to respond favourably, and if this provides them with the opportunity to participate in an activity that particularly appeals to them, so much the better.

If the first contact is by letter, whether directly to the personality or to a gatekeeper, this should cover no more than two pages, preferably only one, of carefully worded text, which is both friendly and informative and which will appeal to the individual concerned. If the first approach is to be by telephone, then write the letter anyway to use as an *aide-mémoir* so as to avoid unnecessary verbiage.

If the person making the approach is not a member of the charity, they will also need to be briefed on the work you do and the reason why the personality's help is so necessary. The person who is to make contact should likewise be motivated and inspired by the work of the charity so that this personal passion will be conveyed.

The response

Having made the approach, you will no doubt be anxiously awaiting a reply – checking emails hourly, searching through the post and answering the phone at the first ring. Not a good idea since it is unwise to depend upon a quick reply. Many celebrities will be unable to say yes without first checking on what professional engagements they are likely to be undertaking in the future, and whether or not their agent, PA or partner feels these will conflict with what you are asking them to do.

The most satisfactory outcome of the approach will be the personality's enthusiastic agreement to your request – you're in business. The worst-case scenario is a definite refusal – in which case you should respect that, thank them for listening and cross them off your list. However, as we all know, there are many shades of grey between black and white:

- The personality says that he/she is very committed to another charity and can't take on another. Reply, expressing understanding and wishing them a continuing and happy association with the charity concerned.

- They say they are very busy right now but might be able to help at some time in the future. Thank them and say that you hope it will be appropriate to send them newsletters from time to time – and do so.

- They don't want to do what you are asking but offer to do something else instead. Unless their alternative offer is for something which is totally wrong for your charity, accept gratefully – it could be the start of a beautiful friendship.

- They express interest and would like to know more. Send them more information together with an offer to meet or an invitation to visit a project and then play it by ear.

Finally, as we have seen, the process of recruiting the help of a personality should involve careful consideration of what help is needed, who would be best able to provide it, how to approach them and how to deal with their response. Such a process is designed to ensure a good and lasting relationship, which will be in the best interests of both the charity and the personality.

Checklist for the approach

- Prepare some basic information on the work of your charity
- Be pragmatic about why they might be interested in helping you
- Explain just how their involvement will help your cause
- Tell them which other public figures are supporting you
- Be clear and truthful about what you want them to do
- Unsolicited approaches from a stranger seldom succeed
- Don't depend upon a quick reply.

CASE STUDY

The Encephalitis Society

The Encephalitis Society is a comparatively small national charity providing information and support for sufferers of a serious brain condition, afflicting both children and adults. The effects of encephalitis can be life-changing both for the people affected and for those caring for them. Add to this the fact that the symptoms are frequently difficult to understand for those with no experience of the condition. and it may be seen why the charity was anxious to exercise extreme care in selecting a patron.

Various names were considered – MPs, high-ranking members of the clergy and others – but none of those put forward had personal experience of the devastating effects of encephalitis. With the best will in the world they would have lacked the understanding and empathy, which the charity deemed so essential in a patron.

For some years there had been a name buzzing round the head of Ava Easton, the charity's development manager, but she had convinced herself that he would not want to be involved. The personality concerned met all the requirements in that, having suffered two brain tumours in the nineties, he knew the fear and trauma that goes with the experience of neurological illness and disability. He was also well known and popular among a large section of the public, and was un-associated with the kind of adverse publicity that affects many celebrities from the world of pop music and television soap shows. There was no doubt about it: Martin Kemp ticked all the boxes.

Having decided that an approach must be made, Ava embarked upon her research, reading Martin's autobiography, gathering information from the net and learning all she could about him. Thus prepared, she telephoned Martin's agents to outline the charity's aims and to ask whether he might be interested in lending his support in some way. The agent's office agreed to get back to her, but after three weeks Ava called again to ask if there had been any response. The agents again said they would chase things up and, after a further two weeks, Ava received an email saying that Martin had asked that she be provided with his personal email address. A result!

The next step was to prepare a carefully worded email asking if he might consider becoming the charity's patron, and also to invite him to attend the launch the following year of an information DVD for people affected and their families. Two weeks later Ava's inbox displayed an email from 'sender – Martin Kemp'! With a mixture of fear and hope, she opened the email to find a warm message from Martin, outlining his own neurological experiences and concluding with the words 'it would be an honour to support your charity and I will help in any way I can.' Fearing she had misunderstood, Ava emailed back asking whether that meant he would become the charity's patron to which he replied: 'Of course!'

Ava met Martin a couple of months later to discuss the charity's work and he filmed an introductory piece for their new information DVD. He also attended the DVD launch and, as Ava says: 'he was the first to arrive and virtually the last to leave; he was approachable, had a million photos taken with our members and, during his speech, asked them all to come and speak to him. His attendance meant we got a lot of press interest and this in turn meant raising much-needed awareness of our cause. An unexpected bonus was that he knew exactly how to handle the more aggressive members of the press world and I learned a lot from listening to him.'

Since then, Martin has continued as The Encephalitis Society's treasured Patron and explains just how special this involvement is for him. 'Like many others, I was regularly bombarded with requests to help charities, but I wanted to be connected with a cause that I can relate to; when I speak to people who have a brain injury, my own experience has opened a door for me to be able to understand because I have been through it too.'

An inspiring example of considering whom to approach, dealing with the gatekeepers, getting the message right, managing the response and reaping the benefits!

7

How do you manage them?

- Who's in control?
- Clarifying expectations on both sides
- Providing the necessary support
- Working with intermediaries
- Managing the risks

As every fundraiser is aware, working with volunteers carries its own pleasures, pitfalls, possibilities and problems – and nowhere is this more evident than in relationships with personalities. That charities take the involvement of all volunteers seriously is beyond doubt, as the growing number of volunteer policies witness. And although patrons and presidents are rarely mentioned in these policies, the general principles must apply equally to them. There are, of course, many instances of personalities providing help to charities on a paid basis, but this is outside the scope of this book. A contractual arrangement involving payment is clearly subject to its own legal and other requirements.

When all is said and done, charities need volunteers, and the alliance between charity and volunteer needs to be carefully managed so as to gain maximum benefit from this valuable resource. As in any management situation, the first consideration is ...

Who's in control?

It must be borne in mind that a charity's prime objective must be the advancement of its cause. Anything which detracts from that is to be avoided at all costs. However, it has to be recognised that the relationship between a charity and its high-profile volunteers needs to be one of mutual control in which the charity determines what it wants the personality to do, but the personality decides whether or not they are willing to do it. Therefore, before any relationship can be finalised, it is essential that both parties are very clear as to what exactly is expected.

Clarifying expectations on both sides

Do you know what you want them to do?

In managing your high-level volunteers, have a clear idea of the precise duties which you would like them to perform and talk this through with them. Ensure that you reach a firm agreement about:

- the form of their involvement – in other words, their role;
- the time commitment that is expected from them;
- the back up and support that your charity is to provide;
- the hoped-for outcome of their association with you.

If the personality's help is required for a one-off event or project, the timescale is self-evident but in the case of the roles of patron or president, further clarification is required. The appointment of members of the Royal Family to such roles is normally expected to be on a more or less permanent basis but this does not have to be so in other cases. You might prefer to make the appointment time-limited. This does have certain advantages for both parties, in that it gives protection for you if the personality should fade from the public eye or if he or she becomes controversial in some way. It also relieves the personality from the somewhat daunting commitment of signing up for an ongoing role from which it could be embarrassing to disentangle themselves should their circumstances change. Indeed, some charities have a definite policy of making no long-term appointments – even for patrons and presidents.

Do they know what they are supposed to do?

The importance of a written agreement of some kind cannot be too highly stressed, even if this takes the form of a simple letter confirming what has been agreed in telephone conversations, meetings or emails with the personalities or their agents. Such a letter should serve to clarify the expectations on both sides including such issues as levels of support and PR opportunities.

Some charities feel that any more formally structured agreement is inappropriate, believing that this might be perceived by the personality – or, more likely by their agent – as too restrictive and binding. However, if your personality will be engaging in high-profile activities such as appearing on television on your behalf, it is desirable to have a formal contract in relation to that specific activity.

Age Concern Surrey has a general form of words laid out in letter style which is sent to all their personalities. This provides confirmation of what has been agreed between the parties, what is expected from the personality, what the personality can expect from the charity, the nature of the event or project and, importantly, whether the personality will charge expenses – and, if so, how much.

Breakthrough also adopts a fairly informal approach in most cases, clarifying the nature of the involvement in a letter or email rather than drawing up a fully detailed agreement that they feel may not be acceptable to the personalities. However, written agreements are used in cases such as their Doodle Campaign which could entail questions of copyright or intellectual ownership.

Similarly, The Children's Trust does not insist on written agreements except in cases where the personality is to be involved in a television programme such as *Who Wants to be a Celebrity Millionaire?*

Other issues upon which clarity is essential include:

- when and in what context the charity can use the personality's name;
- the circumstances in which the personality can refer to their association with the charity;
- whether the personality will provide images for fundraising materials;
- the personality's willingness or otherwise to work with the local media, make personal appearances at fundraising events or even go on overseas visits.

When considering the initial agreement, formal or otherwise, remember also that the charity has a responsibility to ensure that personalities are fully briefed, not only about the event or project with which they are to be involved but also about the charity's background and objectives. As observed elsewhere in this book, a well-briefed personality is an invaluable asset but an ill-informed spokesperson can do positive harm to the charity – and bring embarrassment upon him or herself. Briefing should be designed to ensure that the recipient is in possession of all the information needed to demonstrate the charity's values and to speak on its behalf – without complicating the message.

Remember that, in most circumstances, a brief should be just that – brief. It is usually unnecessary and, indeed, undesirable, to include a detailed history of the charity and fully documented expositions of its vision, values and mission statement – unless, of course, it is in this connection that you have requested their help. If, for instance, you ask a personality to provide help in producing written material, it is essential that you have first established that they fully understand not just what is needed but also the context in which it is to be used.

Many years ago, one of the client charities with which I was working was setting up a very locally based regeneration project and had, quite appropriately, recruited some of the leading figures in the community to help get it started – most notable, a very senior Church of England cleric. 'Just the person to write our mission statement', declared the chairman. 'As a clergyman, he'll know all about mission,' which, of course, he did. Pleased to be entrusted with the task, he worked long and enthusiastically to produce the definitive mission statement for the new charity, while the trustees eagerly looked forward to having a carefully crafted sentence to put under the charity's title on the letterhead. When the results of the learned man's devoted labours were eventually presented to the trustees, they proved to consist of three pages of closely written script – beautifully constructed and grammatically perfect but quite unsuitable for the purpose for which it was required. My fault entirely, since I had mistakenly assumed that everyone knew what a mission statement should look like and where it was to be used. Lesson learned: never assume: always explain.

Providing the necessary support

Most charities have a volunteers' policy (and if not, they are strongly advised to do so; Volunteering England provides very helpful pointers regarding this on their website). In some cases, this will be a detailed set of rules formally agreed by the trustees and in others a matter of simple common sense and civility; but we all recognise the need to extend courtesy and assistance to those who provide their time and effort to our cause voluntarily. As a steward for the National Trust, I look forward to the tea and cakes which are provided for the volunteer workforce at intervals during the day, giving as it does an opportunity to rest and chat with my fellow stewards. All of them could afford to stand in the queue and pay for their own refreshments but nevertheless appreciate the courtesy that the Trust extends to its volunteers. It is important to remember that the requirement of good manners and consideration applies to all volunteers, from room stewards at Polesden Lacey to rock stars giving charity concerts at Wembley Arena.

We should never fall into the trap of assuming that personalities belong to a separate category of volunteer for the purposes of the treatment they receive at our hands. Take, for instance, the question of expenses. If the duties which a personality is undertaking for you necessitate an overnight stay, a meal or a journey, it would be unreasonable to assume that, because of their lifestyle, they will expect to bear the cost themselves – unless, of course, they offer to do so. To make such an assumption could well give offence to the personality and embarrassment to the charity. Similarly, it would be unreasonable for the personality to present the charity with an unexpected bill for an overnight stay at the Ritz and the cost of a chauffeur-driven Rolls after a brief visit to one of your projects.

Clearly, the question of expenses is one of the factors that needs to be agreed upon right from the start. But there are other areas of support that charities have a responsibility to provide during a personality's involvement.

Press releases, which concern an event or a project, impact not only upon the charity but also upon any personality mentioned in them. While it is preferable to avoid having to send all press releases to the personality for approval because of the inevitable delay, it has to be recognised that some personalities or, more particularly, their agents, may insist upon this. If so, ensure that the requirement is complied with.

Be clear about the activities involved in an event and the personality's part in them. And during the event itself, look after them. If, for instance, they are to run a charity auction at a ball, they will need to stay sober all evening – as, indeed, will you! Make sure this is the case, thus avoiding embarrassment for all concerned. If you want to introduce them to other guests, ensure that you check this out with them in advance and brief them on whom they are to meet so that they have something to chat about. Remember that not everyone is good at 'small talk' and knowing a little about the person you are talking to helps. Are they to make a speech at the event? If so, do they want you to give them a few points to work on – or would they prefer you to write it for them and send it for approval well in advance? Ask them.

Even if the personality concerned is to 'host' an event, it is your job to assist them in that task by playing host to them, ensuring their comfort throughout the function and, very importantly, ensure that they are able to leave on time – if necessary, by restricting the number of autograph signings and personal approaches from people who wish to meet them. Put simply, 'stand in their shoes' and make their task as comfortable and pleasurable as possible – that way, they might volunteer their services again.

Above all, remember that you have a responsibility to protect two reputations – that of your charity and that of your personality. Neglect either at your peril.

Working with intermediaries

In previous chapters, we have looked at the possibility of using and working with intermediaries in making the approach, particularly in the case of celebrities. A good relationship with an agent or PA can also be of value during an ongoing relationship with a personality. Bear in mind, though, the fact that clarity is as important here as it is in dealing directly with the personality. One fundraiser, who prefers to remain anonymous for obvious reasons, cited as an example an occasion when a celebrity who had agreed to give a concert in aid of her charity suggested she get in touch with his agent to 'confirm details'.

The agent said he would be happy to do so but then explained that his celebrity client would need various support acts which he, the agent, could provide – no doubt from among his other clients – and also stipulated that the charity should book a suitable theatre of his choosing. He subsequently submitted a note of his fees not only for providing the support acts but also for the commission which he would have received if the celebrity had charged his normal performance fee. What was intended as a generous offer of help by the celebrity to the charity turned out to be a very costly affair, leaving a less than benevolent atmosphere hanging over all concerned. With the benefit of hindsight, the fundraiser involved no doubt wishes that she could 'rewind the tape' and inject a little clarity into her initial dealings with the agent concerned!

One fundraising director often makes a point of developing a good relationship with the celebrity's agent/PA/secretary in the early stages but, later on, when trust has been gained, she is able to contact the celebrity directly which saves time when booking dates, arranging transport and so on.

Managing the risks

The Institute of Fundraising's Code of Practice on Volunteers stresses the importance of researching celebrities to establish whether any aspect of their reputation might prove harmful to the organisation's reputation – and of carrying out this research before any approach is made. In other words, if you've done your homework before getting them involved in the first place, you'll be aware of some of the issues that may arise. Nevertheless, you should always be prepared for the unexpected. Skeletons have a nasty habit of jumping out of the closet at precisely the wrong moment.

The celebrity world is by no means static and constant, and it is a sensible precaution to have in hand a contingency plan in case your chosen personality attracts sudden and potentially damaging media attention. The Media Trust advises that you decide under which circumstances to support your celebrity and when to distance your organisation from them. The other side of this coin is, of course, that your charity may begin to attract media attention which, for whatever reason, your personality considers is not compatible with his or her image and decides to sever relationships with you. Either way, the association is no longer mutually beneficial and has therefore run its course.

Of course, the risks are not limited to those surrounding reputation. The whole issue of risk and volunteering has become a major focus in recent years. Risks which have been highlighted include injuries to clients, employees, volunteers and the public. Volunteer-related risks include exceeding boundaries and authority, breach of confidentiality and misrepresenting the organisation. Katharine Gaskin has produced *Risk Toolkit* published by Volunteering England and it is strongly recommended that you work your way through this very useful guide for organisations wishing to provide for risk in volunteering.

Consider carefully what are the potential dangers, risk situations or problems that could occur because of or related to volunteer involvement. It is vitally important that the process of risk management is thoroughly documented and kept under constant review. Having risk management in place is also an important factor in obtaining insurance – especially for events. The British Brokers' Association lists brokers by region and can identify members who have a particular specialism.

Breakthrough puts together a risk document for every event and this forms part of a risk register across every department of the organisation – legal, events, PR, fundraising, operations etc. – and includes the involvement of celebrities and other personalities.

As we have seen, the relationship between charity and personality is, to some extent, one of co-dependency and the possible negative issues include:

- the time, effort and cost entailed in briefing and looking after them;
- the possibility of their losing their high-profile status for whatever reason;
- the risk that they begin to attract unwanted or negative media coverage;
- the chance of possible unreliability due to whatever causes.

On the subject of unreliability, it is important to recognise that this is a particular risk when involving celebrities as volunteers. However great the celebrity's desire to help and commitment to your cause, he or she will have to take into account the pressing requirements of their career. With the best will in the world, filming schedules are frequently changed at short notice; auditions for cherished roles cannot be ignored; theatre or concert dates may be rescheduled and transport arrangements from far-flung places can fall into disarray. Your risk analysis must therefore take this 'unreliability' factor into account and contingency plans should be put in place.

Bearing in mind the fact that some celebrities have diaries which are booked up for years ahead, it would sometimes seem that the only way to be reasonably sure of obtaining a celebrity's presence on a particular date is by obtaining a slot in their calendar well in advance. There is, however, a counter-argument in that there are occasions when a celebrity is more able to give a positive response if asked only a few days or weeks ahead of an event – such as when they find they have an unexpected break in filming or recording schedules, providing a window of opportunity that could not have been foreseen, say, a year in advance.

Miles Denny, fundraising director of Oakhaven Hospice Trust, gives a cautionary warning to those seeking to engage politicians to speak at events. 'I once booked a high-profile politician who was a renowned speaker and had empathy with my charity. She was very popular and genuine and agreed some 14 months in advance to come free of charge. What I had not bargained for was that, on the day of the event, Parliament was sitting and, although she had had no plans to attend the House herself on that day, there was a party whip and she had no option. I was left with 150 paying diners looking forward to hearing her speak and only 24 hours' notice of her enforced cancellation.'

The list of possible risks in involving high-profile volunteers is endless. What, for example, of the situation where your charity is fortunate to have the well-publicised support and help of a popular celebrity couple who subsequently split up? Which one do you want to keep and how do you go about achieving this?

I could go on but we'd all end up with indigestion and throbbing headaches. The important thing is to focus on the relationship with the specific personality you wish to recruit and to consider the risks involved in the relationship you envisage. In addition, remember that charities are not in the business of avoiding risks but of managing them. This involves recognising the potential dangers, allowing for them and making appropriate contingency plans to minimise the effects upon our causes.

Checklist for managing personalities

- Agree what is expected at the outset of the relationship
- Always confirm what has been agreed in writing
- Agree what is appropriate regarding expenses
- Make their task as comfortable and pleasurable as possible
- Consider the possible problems and risks and have a policy in place.

CASE STUDY

From a Celebrity's PA

I have worked in the capacity of personal assistant to various celebrities for over 20 years – stars of film, television and theatre.

One thing that never, ever changes about this job is the request for the celebrity's time in one way or another, and probably the two biggest requests I receive apart from an autograph are 'something from the celebrity that can be auctioned to raise money for a worthwhile cause' or 'for said celebrity to become involved with or be a figure head for a charity'.

Many of the requests to become involved with charities are redirected to me either by the celebrity's agent or by the company he/she works with. I am the last port of call. Sometimes people ring me directly as they've been given my number, and while I am always ready to listen to requests I always ask for them to be put in an email too. Most of the letters from charities come to me in the form of a letter.

Here's what I prefer: an email request will always get a more prompt answer and attention paid to it only because, as I'm working at my desk and it pops onto my screen, I can deal with it relatively quickly. I get so many letters on a weekly basis with regard to my boss: invitations, fan mail, requests for photographs, requests for items to auction, charity requests and stacks of post on any given day, that it can take me a while to get through for obvious reasons. Emails are a quicker more effective way to get someone's attention and I'm always happy to give out my email address.

I'm often asked if my boss will appear somewhere for a charity and it will only take half an hour to an hour or so of his time. Yes, but then I have to take into account that it might take him an hour and a half to get there, things rarely stick to just the half hour, then I have to get him back to where he needs to be. So half an hour or so of his time, effectively ends up being at least half a day. The person I currently work for is exceedingly busy so wanting him to appear within the next two months somewhere is nigh on impossible. As much notice as possible is always appreciated and stands to be more do-able.

There are certain celebrities I know who are patrons of more than one charity and these charities are chosen because usually they're close to their heart for whatever reason. The pull on a well-known person to actively support a charity is so huge because of course their face becomes the face of the worthwhile cause. So what is it that will draw me to pay close attention to a charity in particular? I'll tell you:

- a clearly laid out email stating as succinctly as possible the aims of the charity;
- what would be expected of my boss in terms of time and commitment;
- why the charity thinks my boss would be a good patron.

I'm always impressed if people have done their homework and not just want him because 'he's very popular and will bring great attention to the cause' but want him because they believe he'll be the right man for the job.

Reasons why he would be an invaluable choice, apart from his fame, would show that great thought has been put into the initial contact with me and it behoves them greatly when I forward their request on to him. Having the right famous person heading up your charity could be supremely beneficial for your cause. Target the person you feel fits the bill best. Go directly to the PA if you can. If you truly believe that the celebrity you've approached is the right person, and you don't hear back for a couple of weeks, then re-send the email. It doesn't help to pester, but a gentle reminder tactfully executed is always worth a try.

8

Ongoing relationships

- Till death us do part?
- Recognising their contribution
- Staying in touch

Till death us do part?

'Life is just one damned thing after another.' (Elbert Hubbard 1859–1915)

The above quotation nicely sums up the ever-changing nature of the situations that life presents to us. Nothing remains constant forever. But an often-quoted maxim in my family is: 'everything should be regarded as permanent until, for whatever reason, it ceases to be so.' Thus, relationships with personalities in connection with our charities should be treated as ongoing and stable until circumstances make it appropriate to move on – by which time suitable contingency plans should be already in place.

Examples abound of charity/personality relationships that have been sustained very successfully for many years. HRH Princess Royal's involvement with Save the Children began in 1970 when she was 20 years of age and the association continues 38 years later. No doubt Centrepoint hopes this pattern will continue with the appointment of her nephew, Prince William who was only 23 when he became their patron in 2005.

The well-known alliance between Mencap and Brian Rix first began in the 1950s when he became involved in fundraising for them, for which he was awarded the CBE in 1977, going on to be appointed secretary-general in 1980, chairman in 1988 and now as Lord Rix, he is their president.

Such lifetime commitments are of very great benefit to the charities, resulting in a vast amount of publicity, increased income and therefore the advancement of their charitable objectives. In each case, the relationship has been carefully nurtured and valued by both charity and personality on an ongoing basis to the great advantage of the cause. Long may these alliances continue. But even in strong and ongoing partnerships, we must beware the illusion of 'permanency'. The circumstances of either the charity or the personality can – and ultimately will – change and render it necessary or appropriate to move on in the interests of either or both. However, in any close relationship, each party is likely to be aware of the other's position, and changes in circumstances should come as no surprise, allowing departures to be planned so as to be handled in the best possible way for all concerned.

When beginning a relationship with a personality, charities need to consider what degree of 'permanency' is to be envisaged. In the case of Royal patrons, it is perhaps reasonable to assume that the appointment is to be long-lasting – and indeed it usually is. Nonetheless, there are other classes of personality who may also wish an ongoing association with a particular organisation – particularly those who have a deeply felt personal affinity to the cause and a genuine desire to help in any way they can on an ongoing basis. The example given above of Lord Rix is a case in point. However, while such offers of help are welcome and potentially of immense value to the charity concerned, the most effective way forward is usually the 'step-by-step' approach, giving both parties the opportunity of reviewing the roles and deciding whether or not the arrangement is working or could more usefully take a different form.

Such a 'step-by-step' basis is sensible in the case of new relationships involving personalities of all types, bearing in mind that, with the best will in the world, not all turn out as planned. This need not be through any 'falling-out' but simply with the passage of time. The popularity of celebrities can decline as well as increase; politicians can lose their seats or resign; eminent professionals, whether in the field of science, medicine or the arts, may take on other roles, move abroad or retire. Such life changes may not necessarily bring the involvement with your charity to an end but will almost certainly mean that it alters in character.

Another factor to keep in mind is that if your personality is attractive to your charity, he or she is likely to be equally so to others, some of whom may engage the personality's interest to the extent of diluting, or indeed extinguishing, their relationship with you altogether. This is said, not to induce paranoia but to highlight again the need to be aware of possibilities and to follow the example of the founder of The Scout Association, Lord Baden-Powell – 'Be prepared!'

Of course, not all charity/personality relationships are intended to be long-lasting. As we have seen in previous chapters, it is common for high-profile individuals to be recruited for one-off events or projects without any obligation on their part to continue the association. However, such cases can fall into the 'step-by-step' category in that, depending upon the success or otherwise of the event, there may be opportunities for further involvement, either in future one-off projects or in more formal and sustained roles. Sometimes chance meetings can turn into beautiful and lasting friendships.

Death is usually considered to be pretty final in the general scheme of things. And yet, as in many other areas, the charity world sometimes proves an exception to the rule. There are a number of charities whose founders made such a contribution to the cause that their influence and inspiration live on after their death. Obvious examples are Group Captain Leonard Cheshire, Sue Ryder, Thomas Barnado and the 7th Earl of Shaftesbury. Indeed, the charities they founded still bear their names with pride.

Recognising their contribution

Charities are well aware of the importance of providing recognition for the contributions made by those who give their services on a voluntary basis. However, the form which that recognition should take sometimes requires a little consideration. We know that everyone who volunteers their help deserves thanks – irrespective of the form that help takes or at what level it is provided – but there are many ways of saying 'thank you', ranging from a simple letter setting out the ways in which the charity has benefited from their work in running a stall at a local bring-and-buy sale to a fundraising reception given in their honour.

There are many other methods of providing the recognition that is deserved.

There are, for instance, a growing number of annual awards organised within the charity sector by various umbrella bodies or trade organisations. Check to find out whether any of these provide an opportunity for you to acknowledge publicly the high value you place upon the contribution that your key leaders have made to your charity. Those concerned will gain encouragement and satisfaction from knowing that their services are valued and, as a useful by-product, your charity will also benefit from the resulting publicity. Some examples of suitable awards are given in the box below.

Charity sector annual awards

- The Charity Awards
  The Award for Outstanding Achievement (www.charityawards.co.uk)
- Third Sector's Britain's Most Admired Charity Awards
  Celebrity Charity Champion (www.thirdsector.co.uk)
- The Institute of Fundraising National Awards
  Volunteer Fundraiser of the Year (www.nationalawards.org.uk).

Remember that appointment to the role of patron, president or vice-president can itself provide a form of recognition for commitment already shown to your cause. The Children's Trust, for example, appointed their vice-presidents for this purpose. For comparatively new charities, this can be an appropriate way of rewarding the chair of the first trustees upon his or her standing down after the formative period. This happened in two charities with which I was involved in their early years.

Of course, there is also the Honours List – always remembering that it would be unwise to promise what you can't in fact deliver. There are many examples of personalities of all categories having achieved success in their own field but not actually receiving honours for their contribution to the voluntary sector. It is not within the scope of this book to examine the merits or otherwise of this system, nor to explain how to go about using it. Suffice it to say, do not lose sight of the possibility regardless of your own view – it is your personality's view that counts here.

Whichever way you choose to acknowledge publicly the services of your high-level volunteers, never forget the most important factor of all – your own personal appreciation of their contribution. No matter how we study, analyse or categorise personalities, we must never lose sight of the fact that, beneath the public persona, each is a private individual who, like any of us, will respond best to other individuals with whom they have a friendly relationship. Valuable as recognition mechanisms are, in the final analysis, strong and lasting alliances have far more to do with warm, personal understanding and simple friendship.

Staying in touch

As we all know, friendship is something that needs to be worked at. The staunchest and most amicable relationship will founder unless it is nourished and kept alive. How many times have we all said: 'do you remember old so-and-so? I wonder how he's getting on these days.' By that time, it's usually too late to re-establish contact. Old so-and-so has moved on and probably forgotten us – and yet we used to be so close. What went wrong? We didn't keep in touch, that's what went wrong.

In the euphoric early stages of our charity's contact with a personality, practically all our energies are directed to developing the relationship – and the ways to do this are usually fairly obvious. If the individual concerned laid the foundation stone for a new building, we can invite them to the grand opening when it is completed; if they have spearheaded a direct mail campaign, we can let them know how much was raised as a result. But what do we do then? Do we let the relationship quietly fade away until it's too late to re-establish contact – to the point where they have moved on and, like old so-and-so, forgotten us?

Of course we don't. What about inviting the foundation-stone layer to the celebration of the first and subsequent anniversaries of the opening of the new building? Wouldn't it be courteous to contact the personality who featured in the direct mail campaign and send snippets from any encouraging letters received from donors? How about sending press articles – not just those in which the personality is mentioned but whenever the charity attracts media coverage? Keep them informed about the work that their participation helped make possible. Let them know if the charity is to be mentioned on a television or radio programme or interview. On a more personal note, why not send them Christmas and birthday cards or good wishes on special family occasions? If they are ill or in hospital, wouldn't they appreciate some flowers with a personal note to let them know you're thinking of them? They are, after all, your 'best friends' – or should be.

The importance of this 'personal' aspect of the charity/personality relationship cannot be too highly stressed. Because of this, it is vital to decide who will be their key contact within the organisation. This will quite possibly be the person who recruited them in the first place, although staff changes occur and it will be important to ensure a timely 'hand-over' of the relationship. If you are the contact and are leaving, let them know. Don't wait for a stranger to get in touch with them saying they have taken over from you.

In the case of patrons and presidents, especially members of the Royal Family, it is usual for these relationships to be managed by the chief executive's office – in which case, it is essential that all other departments within the charity are aware of this and ensure that the appropriate channels of communication are maintained.

One last thing – if you already have a successful relationship with a personality, who better to help or advise you on bringing others on board? After all, their circle of acquaintances will almost certainly include other equally well-known figures, and their influence will extend into the very places you need to reach to attract these high-profile people to your charity. What is more, their understanding of what's involved in obtaining support from personalities is unsurpassed – the nature of personalities; their suitability for roles within your organisation; which personalities would be good for you and how to identify them; how to approach them and get them on board; the kind of management they would respond to . . . But this is, I think, where we came in.

Let's keep in touch.

Checklist for a lifetime relationship

- Keep faith with the agreement
- Be clear about expectations
- Provide professional support
- Keep them informed on the bad news as well as the good
- Recognise their contribution
- Thank them
- Thank them
- Thank them.

CASE STUDY

The Children's Trust

Elaine Paige OBE, first visited The Children's Trust in Tadworth, Surrey when she was representing The Variety Club and came to present a minibus to the charity. She toured the centre and was really moved by the courage of the children and the work of the staff, and returned later on a private visit, armed with presents for the children.

She began to take a close interest in the work; attending sessions in the therapy centre and taking part in assemblies at the school, joining in with the children who really loved hearing her sing. Elaine was made a vice-president as a way of recognising her significant commitment to the charity and in 1999 she presented another minibus.

Director of fundraising, Liz Haigh-Reeve, explains just what the involvement of Elaine Paige means to the Trust. 'Elaine really understands the importance of raising awareness of our work and always mentions us whenever she gets a chance. For example, she gave an interview in *Hello!* magazine when the Trust was selected to benefit from GMTV's Get Up and Give which prompted several donations including one from the stage at the Palladium where Elaine was performing. We've also had mentions on her radio programme, including a 'hello' to volunteers in our shops and to other supporters, which really inspires them.

'A clay pigeon shoot regularly raises a great deal of money for the Trust – hosted by Elaine to which many celebrity friends are invited – and this provides an opportunity to make new friends. The CLA Game Fair has chosen the Trust to be the benefiting charity in 2008.

'A concert, which Elaine gave in aid of the Trust in Redhill, generated supporters at every level, including companies who were brought in through the event, and the mayor chose the Trust as his charity of the year.

'Whenever Elaine has a series of concerts or is performing in a play, she includes a special reception for the Trust, and the charity maximises this opportunity by selling a package which includes best seats at the performance as well as a chance to meet Elaine after the show. These are always popular and lucrative fundraising events.

'If the charity is asked to bring along a celebrity to a corporate event, Elaine is always willing to help if she is free and attended the ICAP Charity Day, helping dealers raise extra funds and making their day by singing 'Memory' down the phone to encourage the international traders to pledge funds. This raised £90,000 in funds and excellent PR as a result.

'Together with Michael Ball, Elaine took part in an edition of *Celebrity Who Wants to be a Millionaire?* resulting in a donation of £32,000 for the Trust as well as a similar amount for Michael's chosen charity.'

As Liz says, 'The relationship with Elaine has deepened over the years and gone beyond a working partnership – the children at the Trust are very important to Elaine and we really regard her as part of the family at The Children's Trust.'

Appendix 1

Issues to Consider When Volunteers are Celebrities

The following is taken from the Institute of Fundraising Volunteer Fundraising Code of Practice. To view the full Code of Fundraising Practice visit:
http://www.institute-offundraising.org.uk/bestpractice/thecodes/codesof fundraisingpractice

- Organisations *ought* to have a written celebrity involvement policy, which includes involvement of celebrities as volunteers and in a paid capacity.
- Organisations *ought* to have a written agreement with celebrity supporters, which might take the form of a letter of confirmation from the charity to the celebrity.
- Organisations *ought* to research celebrities and consider whether any aspect of the celebrity's reputation might prove harmful to the organisation's reputation before making any approach.
- Organisations *should* consider the appropriateness of the celebrity for the fundraising activity proposed and issues relating to the desired length and depth of the relationship with the celebrity.
- Organisations *should* clarify and document the benefits and main purpose of involving celebrities in their fundraising on a case by case basis.
- Organisations *should* clarify the expectations of the charity and the celebrity including levels of support and PR opportunities.

- Organisations *ought* to provide the celebrity with a full briefing on the organisation and the activity with which they will be involved.
- Organisations *should* consider the risk to a fundraising event involving celebrities as volunteers should those celebrities not turn up.

Appendix 2

Contact details for case study charities

- www.barnardos.org.uk
- www.meru.org.uk
- www.breakthrough.org.uk
- www.parkinsons.org.uk
- www.encephalitis.info
- www.thechildrenstrust.org.uk
- www.volunteering.org.uk

Index